MY SHYNESS, MY SELF

Learn to Live with Shyness

Fausto Manara

Translated by Allan Cameron

'an association in which the free development of each
is the condition of the free development of all'

FREE ASSOCIATION BOOKS / LONDON / NEW YORK

First published in 2000 by
Free Association Books Limited
57 Warren Street, London W1T 5NR

Copyright © 2000 Fausto Manara

Translation copyright © 2000 Allan Cameron

The right of Fausto Manara to be identified as the author of this work has been asserted by him in accordance with the Copyright, Designs and Patents Act 1988.

ISBN 1 85343 529 5 pbk

A CIP catalogue record for this book is available from the British Library

09   08   07   06   05   04   03   02   01   00
10   9   8   7   6   5   4   3   2   1

Designed, typeset from disk and produced for the publisher by Chase Publishing Services
Printed in the European Union
by Athenaeum Press, Gateshead, England

Contents

Stories of Shy People

Preface

Examples of shyness are to be found everywhere. They are not the sole domain of psychiatrists and psychotherapists, even though a great many shy people are to be found in their case studies, ranging from those who seek help specifically for this problem to those who hide it under a myriad of other clinical forms and symptoms. These, of course, include some of the courageous shy people, who are tired of bluffing and can no longer put up with the terrible weight of trying to live their lives like giants when they feel like dwarfs. Some are tired of blushing when they would like to look inscrutable, some can no longer stand feeling the beads of sweat standing out on their forehead when they would like to behave with cool detachment, and some are enervated by the anxiety they feel at the approach of even the most run-of-the-mill appointment.

And there are many, many others, as I can vouch from my own clinical experience. Each one would ask me for special help with a different problem from his or her fellow sufferers, but with a common root: the unsuccessful struggle against their own shyness. That shyness not only manifested itself in relation to other people, but also in relation to life itself.

But, as I said, you do not just come across such shy people in a psychiatrist's consulting room. They are to be seen in many places – in all places – perhaps without it being possible to detect their well-camouflaged shyness. They are a great multitude that more or less corresponds to the whole of humanity.

Shyness is a very human sentiment. It is a sentiment that most people consider shabby or ignoble when they recognize it in another person, and their reaction is one of aggression rather than under-standing or compassion. When they recognize it in themselves, on the other hand, their reaction is not only one of fear and self-pity but also of panic or intolerance. Only very rarely do we react with indulgence, almost never with appreciation.

In other words, shyness is seen as a kind of chronic and crippling illness. It is a monster of varying dimensions with which we feel we have to do battle, but the chances of victory are very small. Yet we do not live in an era like that of the Romantics when even the heroes could occasionally allow themselves to blush without feeling out of place. Nor do we live in the Middle Ages, when knights could openly display their anxiety during the fretful wait for their loved-one to say yes. It hardly needs saying that there is ample evidence that until very recent times shyness was considered a virtue in women.

No, we live in a very different period that is competitive, technological and pushy, a period in which the control of emotions is *de rigueur*. There are a few exceptions, such as those talk-shows where the expression of feelings is greeted with excitement and applause, but everything is underwritten by a truth that appears to be fiction and within a preconceived framework, so that when the credits come up the imperative of self-control is immediately reimposed.

Yet shyness is part of the connective tissue of human characteristics. It is certainly its most widespread feature, in spite of being unjustly considered an area close to the pathological. Clearly it manifests itself more sharply in situations where the social requirements of a given culture put it on a kind of list of proscribed emotions. It is no coincidence that in the Western world a copious literature on the subject has flourished and the Internet has been flooded with information on it.

The insane crusade against shyness has created an industry: courses in assertiveness, handbooks that teach you how to overcome the 'problem' in ten easy moves, the myth of fitness, the image-changing treatments of plastic surgery, drugs and finally the ever-so-American 'shy-clinics' (for the clinical treatment of shyness) where you go in weak and come out strong. If only! All this amounts to is money – up to thousands of dollars – and the failure to accept part of yourself as precisely that, part of yourself.

In twenty years of clinical experience, I have encountered a host of people whose problems arose from their lack of success in their struggle against shyness. I increasingly asked myself whether all that effort made sense, and I tried to put the same question to my patients. The reply was a categorical 'no'. There is another route that can be taken in order to get more out of life, one that uses fewer resources and is more respectful of ourselves. This is the route I propose to chart in this book.

We will go through the various phases in the development of shyness. These are not peculiar phenomena, but the shared rational and evolved destiny of the great majority of us. We will examine how social expectations, which are always very high, can profoundly unsettle us. We can thus discover how the persistent and unsuccessful suppression of shyness can generate genuine and significant psychiatric pathologies, such as social phobia. The consideration of this aspect will be the first opportunity to reflect upon the risks of fighting an enemy that in reality is a central part of our own individuality.

We will then observe the results of the efforts made to disguise it without, however, eradicating it. Everyone will recognize something of themselves, but shouldn't feel guilty or that they are a suitable case for treatment. These are common, almost universal expedients, although the strategies differ. We will look into the relationship between shyness and sexuality, in a chapter that illustrates the risks of 'having to be' and 'having to do'. Relapses can have harmful effects on the way couples live together.

We will conclude with an alternative theory and proposal to the strategies that are commonly adopted in order to overcome this state of mind. My failure to be more specific at this stage does not arise from any desire to leave the reader in suspense, but is simply because I do not want to run the risk of over-simplification. My arguments will not only be theoretical: along the way I will try to touch on some experiences we have all shared. It will be a journey in which those of us who feel small will be able to find some useful tips on how to get the upper hand without having to undergo strain and without fighting with ourselves, as is commonly the case.

The Coat

I was fifteen years old and lived in Cantù, a small town in the province of Como where the traditions of lace-making were dying out and affluence began to spread through the workshops producing quality furniture. I grew up in a family that came from the country-side, and my parents maintained their links with the countryside by trading in agricultural produce. I went to the second year of *liceo* in the only school in the town where this was possible. It was a Catholic school and of course private, frequented by the sons and daughters of well-to-do families who were both local and from other parts of the region. Some even came from as far away as Milan. My social background caused me some difficulties. It wasn't that there was anything unpleasant in my relations with my fellow students, but when parties or gatherings were organized in the houses of the rich and important of the town, I did face a few problems. Within the class system, invitations to me, the son of a greengrocer, were not unheard-of but neither were they plentiful.

One winter's day, a school-friend who came from one of the prominent families invited me to his birthday party. Of course I was delighted. My mother prepared my best clothes and at eight o'clock I went smartly dressed to their magnificent house. Concerns over my genealogy did not even occur to me. I remember that during the evening I courted a young girl, whose name regretfully escapes me, and she returned my attentions. Being the son of a poorer family did not appear to bar the way to the tiny jet-set of a provincial town. Indeed I had managed to worm my way in so well as to be preferred over all the others by the beautiful girl (or so I like to remember her).

While I was enjoying myself, it got to one o'clock and we prepared to go home. It was much later than I or the majority of young people were used to in the early sixties. Given that my potential loved-one had already been collected by her parents half an hour earlier, I chatted for a while with the remaining guests in the large entrance hall. Just then Alessandro (whose name, unlike the girl's, I can still remember) passed by and said goodbye to me. I knew him to be one of the wealthiest guests at the party. I couldn't help observing him as he left and thinking, who knows why, that he had a really smart coat, the smartest I had ever seen. We continued our conversation for a while and then Alessandro reappeared at the front door with this coat in his hand. He held it up and said, 'This isn't mine, I made a mistake when I collected it from the cloakroom.' A few seconds passed before I realized the truth: that beautiful coat was in fact mine. Its attractiveness had only struck me when worn by someone else. It had to be on another person's shoulders before I could attribute it with a certain quality, an excessive quality which was not entirely its own, as though it had magically started to sparkle.

In life you come across many such episodes that throw a powerful light on things that are not what they seem and things that are much more than we suppose. At the age of fifteen, I was not yet able to grasp its full meaning. It was simply a pleasant surprise. That coat has accompanied me throughout my life, and has made me see things more clearly. It taught me to evaluate things more carefully, and not to delegate to potential Alessandros the role of making something look beautiful whose beauty is only personal wealth.

In short, that episode taught me more than the lengthy period of psychoanalytical training that I was to go through much later. The coat had thrown light on a symptom of shyness in its formative stage. It had revealed it. It had exposed a failure to understand that qualities shouldn't be perceived as positive in others and outmoded in oneself.

Part One

The Birth of Shyness and its Evolution

1   The Origins

Although it is the cause of much unease for those who experience it, shyness has, if you think carefully, a certain gentleness about it, almost as though gentleness and shyness go together. Indeed, there has been a tradition that maintained this by associating it almost exclusively with the female sex. It is however more common to adopt an irritable, even bitter, tone in relation to this feeling and way of perceiving ourselves relating to others, and the root causes for this are to be found in the history of the individual. It is a history in which the emotional bookkeeping often ends up with a deficit as a result of the credit entries that have never been collected (and are no longer collectable), and this can cause aggressive tendencies (to some extent against others, but much more against oneself).

This is why shyness can easily diverge from its potential gentleness. It takes on connotations of a kind of shame when it comes to putting oneself forward. It becomes full of negative feelings that make it seem like guilt. It matters little that it does not correspond to any objective reality in life as it is experienced. It is, in fact, a profound and ancient emotion that is difficult to control and does not allow simple responses to apparently trifling problems. Why do we approach unexceptional experiences with so much anxiety? Why are we embarrassed, and why do we feel guilty in such circumstances? What are we embarrassed about? What do we feel guilty about?

'Nothing' could be the reply if it were possible to consider the situation objectively. Yet the opposite inevitably occurs. It is something you cannot escape, in spite of the strenuous defence that you try to put up or your attempts at safeguarding yourself by adopting a critical position that affirms: 'Careful! Don't fall into that trap again – remember your own worth!' But reasoning is rational and can be exercised in periods of calm, whereas emotions are ways of feeling that are

experienced in the heat of the moment. When shyness strikes in the
fevered tension of a given situation, coldness is felt within. It is a sense
of loss and pervasive solitude that takes your breath away, trips up
your speech, colours your cheeks red, makes you move clumsily,
triggers a tic or has you feeling lost in a threatening land where
everyone is a potential aggressor and no one can come to your aid.

Unconscious dynamics are those that cause loss of control, loss of
direction and the need for artificial control, which is however incapable of rediscovering the direction that has been lost. These are
ancient deposits that are encrusted in the most hidden and intimate
parts of our being. They remain silent, and then suddenly appear to
sensational effect, without any warning. This is an inner event that
causes us to lose any sense of the relative wholeness we may have
enjoyed in previous periods of our life, when, for once, we felt happy,
proud of ourselves and reconciled with our existential dimension.

These unconscious dynamics, that are structured from the very
beginning of our personal experiences, draw sustenance from the
direction of our psychological development. The British psychoanalyst Michael Balint has produced a theory that could even be
considered a study of the genesis of shyness. In his 'Basic Fault:
Therapeutic Aspects of Regression', written in 1968, he examines the
question of a very particular inadequacy that the majority of
humanity finds itself experiencing from the very early stages of its life
and becomes the cause of shyness first in childhood, then in adolescence and finally in adulthood. Balint argues that

> you can trace the origin of this basic fault back to the considerable
> divergence that can exist between an individual's needs during his
> or her first two years – the formative years – (or even the first few
> months) and the care it received during that period. This diver-
> gence creates a state of deficiency whose consequences are only
> partially reversible. Although the individual can achieve a good or
> even excellent adaptation, the traces of his very early experience
> remain and intervene in what we call his constitution, individuality
> or the formation of his character.

For the psychoanalyst, the origin of the basic fault depends ultimately on the discrepancy between the child's needs and the care
(material and psychological), attention and love available to its
demands. Indeed every child that comes into the world should be
protected by a kind of 'constitutional charter' of its rights. However,
in spite of being totally dependent and defenceless, babies do not

always receive what they need and are entitled to. They do not need to suffer severe neglect. It may be that the parents, who nevertheless love the baby, cannot be as solicitous as they should for practical reasons, such as work or actual contingent difficulties like illness. But how can very small babies understand that the reason for what they are lacking is not due to any ill-will towards them, but instead to accidents of circumstance? They certainly aren't capable of assessing what is happening around them. They suffer only for what they should have and don't receive. In the first two years of life, babies lay the foundations for the development of their own self-image. They form vague subjective and symbolic truths based on experiences that are often minor and apparently insignificant.

'If our mothers did not have much milk or a nipple from which it was difficult to suckle', writes the psychologist Arthur Wassmer,

> we can develop the sensation that others do not have much to offer us. If our parents were in the habit of shouting and being violent, we might conclude that the world is a violent and unstable place. If we fall from our parents' arms, we may generalize that we cannot put much trust in others. If we had the experience of feeling momentarily suffocated by a breast or a body, we may end up fearing physical closeness.

It would certainly be difficult, if not impossible, to link something that occurs in adulthood by pure reason to these or other similar events, when a later stage in life will also give signs of being imbued with them, just as it is imbued with events that the child experiences a little later in the period from two to five years, when beginning to be a protagonist in his or her own growth.

In this stage relationships with others, particularly parents, become crucial. The attitude that they display can condition the evolution of the child's personality: either it feels equipped and worthy of a central role in social contexts or, conversely, deserving of neglect and abandonment. It is precisely at this point that the mechanism is triggered that engenders feelings of inferiority, inadequacy and failure that will be experienced first as an adolescent and then as an adult. At the very least such feelings will cause the individual concerned to live as a shy person. This mechanism can be illustrated in explicit terms as follows: 'Why don't my parents give me what I want? It has to be because they don't love me.' If this is the case for a baby, so dependent for all its needs, what hope is there? 'Clearly they do not give me what I need because I am not what I should be, because I have some defect, and because I lack something that would encourage them to be more attentive towards me.'

In reality, a small baby cannot follow through this reasoning, but what is formed in its psychological structure and deposited in its unconscious follows a logic that does not diverge a great deal from such hypothetical considerations. Thus the parents' responsibility is taken away, the certainty of their love is maintained on trust (necessarily so) and the responsibility for the inadequate care suffered is turned against oneself, as an inadequate and defective being. This is the basic fault. How often do children as adults live in the hope of some sign that their parents appreciate who they are or what they may have done, by adapting to the family values?

All this is very relevant to shyness, especially in the formative years when the 'essence' of the individual's potential has not been developed in itself and for itself; rather much greater importance has been given to 'being' at least one of a certain type of adjective, such as: 'good, clever, obedient, capable' and so on. Alexander Lowen, in his book *Joy*, stresses this aspect:

> The only conclusion that can be drawn from the observation of parents and children is that it is rarely a question of 'mummy knows best', but rather a question of authority and obedience. A child has to be taught to obey its parents, because they fear that otherwise they would lose control and it would turn against them. This fear does not take into account the fact that a child is a social being whose spontaneous actions are self-expressive and not self-destructive.

I am not interested in following up the pedagogic implications of this consideration. What does interest me however is how much a child is impeded from expressing itself, a factor that will increase its likelihood of being afflicted by shyness in adolescence and adulthood. How can the child that has to be good, clever, obedient or capable, assert something of itself outside the strictures imposed by the straitjacket 'You must do this!' But what is this? It is your parents' impositions then and the social and cultural norms now. You must live up to their expectations. But what expectations are these? 'The expectations that we have laid down.' Thus attempts to assert oneself, to say 'I am here' can only be expressed if one is willing to pay a high price. Once they become adults, such individuals who have been suffocated by the basic fault, guilt and shame, will find that their relationship with the world will not have any firm footholds nor any solid references for perceiving and becoming aware of their own personal capabilities.

The feelings of guilt and shame are fundamental characteristics of shyness although not, as we shall see, exclusive to it. However they have different psychological and psychodynamic preconditions. Guilt insinuates itself into our self-perception in relation to the world when we are affected by a desire or profound need to transgress some external norm, creating anxiety over not being sufficiently compliant with the profound psychological mechanism that Freud defined as the super-ego. It represents the series of norms that a higher entity has inscribed and to which we must conform: ethical, moral and social norms that should meet with our total obedience.

Shame, on the other hand, arises from the acute sense of the discordance between what we should be and what we feel we ought to be. In psychoanalysis, it is said that the feeling of shame manifests itself when we are incapable of living at our ideal level of the ego (an ideal model to which we try to conform), and we are subjected to an inner tension caused by the realization of not having achieved our aim, of having failed not only in the enterprise undertaken but also in the attempt to get closer to the ideal ego. We have failed to be what we ought to be but cannot be. Every time we want someone to like us, we can experience shame when we feel that we have not achieved that aim, and that we are inadequate for the requirements that the situation appears to demand of us. This means that we can experience shame, guilt and shyness when we give up on ourselves and fail to take into consideration our own value and qualities, as though deprived of our senses by anxiety over our deficiencies and the inability they give us to get the upper hand.

According to Freudian theory, shame relates to another dimension: the sexual one. It represents nothing more than the fear of ridicule, a particular kind of symptom (a precursor of other symptoms) that originates from trauma, frustration over the satisfaction of needs and an attempt to defend oneself from sexual instincts. The very same instincts that can give rise to self-accusation in a child for having given room during infancy to some form of sexuality. The sense of shame restricts the openings by which a child can give vent to its own sexual impulses. The origin of shyness and the manner in which we react to it can be seen in the theory of the psychoanalyst Heinz Kohut. When studying narcissism in particular, he distanced himself a little from Balint by asserting that this feature of the personality is generated in a child not solely because of what is provided or not provided by the parents (warmth, love and care), but also as a result of the intensity of its particular needs and impulses. Thus the child might not only excessively idealize the image of the parental figure, but also develop an inflated self-image: a grandiose self, as Kohut defines it.

The excessive idealization of oneself and one's parents can therefore create the basis for a future comparison with the reality that gradually reveals itself to the individual in question, which is so stark as to cause first disillusionment and then fear, critical self-analysis and finally shyness. This also means that narcissistic reactions, consisting of extreme efforts to fulfil or even exceed potential at all costs, are nothing more than a defence and compensatory quest for an unachievable ideal that can only provoke feelings of inadequacy and failure. Inhibited sexuality, a sense of guilt over not being as capable as appears necessary, a need for love (the basic fault) inadequacy in relation to what one should ideally be and frustrated narcissism: these are the ingredients of a mixture which later, when agitated by the demands of a very demanding society, will lead to what we define as shyness.

What if Everything Has Already Been Written?

Apart from the interpretation provided by psychoanalysis, we also need to take into consideration another aspect that determines the way we operate: our temperament. This is a kind of background noise that accompanies our emotional reactions and can be traced back to factors that are not exclusively psychological, but also biological and hereditary.

Attempts to study the roots of human behaviour go back to the times of Hippocrates and particularly Polybus, his adoptive son, who had a theory of humours. This was based on the four elements: earth, water, air and fire, and considered a person's wellbeing to depend on their balance. Hippocrates put a psychological slant on this, and defined four types of behaviour, depending on which of the humours was predominant. We still use the expression 'good-humoured'. At the time of Hippocrates you could have defined your humours as 'sanguine', 'phlegmatic', 'choleric', or 'melancholic'. Times have clearly changed, but temperament is still categorized along these lines, which have been adjusted over the centuries, but whose underlying concept has remained unaltered. That concept is basically that our body interferes with the way we are, even psychologically.

In the revolutionary period of science that witnessed the prominence of Copernicus, Galileo and Harvey, Andreas Rudigher reduced the number of elements that determine temperament to two categories: one responsible for weak qualities and the other for strong qualities. The scientific world saw its knowledge expand and, towards the middle of the eighteenth century, with the commencement of experimental psychology, temperament was shifted from its relationship with blood, bile and various other things, towards a dependence on the nervous system. The question was to be examined by philosophers like Kant (with the differentiation between characteristic and character) and Nietzsche (with the definition of two psychological types: the idealist and the realist), but it was the connection to biology and genetics that came out on top.

Around 1820, Gall and Spurzheim, the founders of so-called phrenology, attempted to introduce a new science according to which an individual's abilities or lack of them corresponded to specific areas of the brain. Actually, they went even further, arguing that there was a clear relationship between the shape and size of the cranium and potential madness. They also included the study of temperament in this system, and theorized the existence of three types: motivated (based on the muscular system), vital (with a predominance of the system that regulates alimentation) and mental (closely dependent on the nervous system).

Since the time of these two German authors up to the present day, this interpretation has become increasingly emphatic to the point of adopting a rather extremist tone. Thus it appears that the individual has little choice but to follow the path mapped out by researchers such as the American psychiatrist Robert Cloninger. A summary of this theory can be found in the book by the psychiatrist Giovanni Battista Cassano, *Liberaci dal male oscuro* (Free Us From The Mysterious Disorder). Its starting-point is the observation that the type of temperament should depend on a few neurotransmitters, the substances that act as messengers and transmit impulses from one nerve cell to the next. The three chemical substances most involved in this are serotonin, dopamine and norepinephrine. The first one's inhibitory role on some forms of human behaviour has been well established. For example, if serotonin activity is reduced, impulsive and aggressive behavioural patterns can increase, whereas if it increases it can inhibit eating and sexual behaviour. The implications of serotonin are particularly significant for mechanisms that trigger anxiety and depression.

Dopamine, on the other hand, has the function of encouraging aggressive behaviour, as well as behaviour directed at exploring the environment, discovering new things and avoiding monotony, and behaviour that stimulates sexual curiosity and the tendency to react in tense relational situations.

Finally, norepinephrine has been shown to affect the regulation of eating behaviour, the rhythm of sleep and wakefulness, the state of vigilance and the control of neurovegetative functions. It is also involved in regulating memory, anxiety mechanisms and reactions to stressful events, and its action, triggered pharmacologically, can be useful in dealing with the symptoms of depression.

Cloninger's temperamental theory is based specifically on the observation of these three biochemical elements. Thus the serotonin system is responsible for the first type of temperament, which makes the individual unwilling to tolerate wrongs. The dopamine system gives rise to the second temperament that motivates the individual to search out innovation. Finally, the norepinephrine system is the cause of the third temperament that conditions the individual to act on the basis of the gratification that he or she hopes to obtain. We can use Cloninger's categories to establish that shy people should belong above all to the first and second types, and enter into social relations either with prudence caused by their concern over suffering painful disappointments or with commitment to behaviour likely to receive the approval of others.

If we then add the assertions made during the eighties and nineties by such researchers as Plomin, Eysenck and Buss, we then have a framework in which types of temperament are not only dependent on chemical substances in the brain, but are also genetically determined. It is claimed (by Buss and Plomin) that some types, such as the ones that lead to introversion, allow extrovert behaviour, or cause the individual to act in a manner not wholly congruous with a healthy relationship with reality, have an inheritance factor of between 40 and 60 per cent. At this stage, the spectre of an inevitable destiny appears to be complete. Shy people, who are very much subject to their own temperament, should hold their own chromosomes responsible for any troublesome or very unpleasant feelings they have to deal with.

It is precisely this kind of dependence that Cassano examines in his previously mentioned book. He defines the shy as having a dysthymic temperament, i.e. the temperament of someone who is 'insecure, timid, habitually complaining, and with low self-esteem'. This is someone who 'tends to brood over things, is aware of his or her limitations and suffers for this, and has difficulty in getting enthusiastic or experiencing pleasure'. The hyperthymic and the cyclothymic are also included in Cassano's categories. The former manifest hyper-vitality and are the bosses or leaders: those who lead and are prepared to command. These are successful people who live in a creative and productive dimension. 'I will describe them', says Cassano. 'They are genial, sensitive, athletic and strong like demigods of the Greek world, equipped with exceptional virtues, extraordinary physical and mental strength, and surpass the others in all skills.' Cyclothymics, on the other hand,

> are always on a seesaw, swinging between depression and expansiveness ... Being fickle and of stormy temperament, they are distinguished by the considerable instability of their affections and work. Many feel the need for strong emotions and hence the tendency for pathological gambling, the use of stimulants, impossible loves, high-risk activities and dependency on alcohol and other substances.

If you look carefully, and we will observe this in greater detail further on, all three categories and not just the dysthymics appear to contain elements, manifestations and symptoms of shyness. Its dependence on biological factors would therefore appear inevitable and inescapable. Hence being shy can only be considered no more and no less than a symptom of a brain disorder.

On this basis, the organicist line of research interprets even the most intimate events in a person's life as of a biochemical rather than a genetic nature. It thus enters a sphere in which an individual's attention to himself, his personal choices and respect for his qualities are subordinate not only to the environment in which he lives but also to his DNA. The system of neurotransmitters that will prevail may already be inscribed in its structure. Substantially, this means that how a child will behave when it grows up has already been predetermined. If this were the case and only if this were the case, every psychological outcome would have already been marked out, including that of being shy. If this were the case, anyone who by chance had a prevalence of the norepinephrine or serotonin systems would only be able to put up with the effects, perhaps by resigning themselves to a life of shyness. There would be little chance of breaking free.

The problem is not, however, one of establishing whether people have a predetermined temperament and have a prevalence of a certain system of neurotransmitters. They are the way they are, because of given biological conditions or because something occurred during their existence that produced a certain effect in the brain. At the moment, neither of the two theories can produce a series of scientific proofs that demonstrate them without a shadow of doubt. As a result of my clinical and human experience, I feel much closer to the second theory.

Even though I have had neurological and therefore organicist training, I have faith in the human potential to govern our own psycho-biological makeup, particularly in the sphere dominated and governed by emotions. These are the colours of our existence, which are determined by a particular situation, event or thought, and depend on the type of reaction we produce. The quality of that emotion hides our history, its roots, all the transitions in the psychological evolution of our affections and sexuality, and the joys and unhappinesses experienced since earliest childhood. There is indeed also the neurotransmitter, which, precisely because of our experiences, develops an excess or deficiency that then becomes a biological marker for shyness.

2 The Different Faces of Shyness

A large part of mankind is covered by the segment that runs from the normal or fairly normal manifestation of shyness (with only the occasional suggestion of a blush) to the frankly pathological forms of shyness (with gestures triggered by fear and panic). As you pass from the former to the latter, there are an increasing number of manifestations, symptoms and psychological traits that may be either subtle or conspicuous. There is, however, a common denominator: fear that others or the public are severe critics of one's own behaviour and appearance. The individual in question ends up subjecting himself to what the psychologist Eugene Sagan calls 'pathological criticism', a kind of negative inner voice that not only judges but is also capable of assault. This critic makes the individual fear that everything he does is wrong and is not worthy of respect, and consequently it imposes unachievable standards of perfection. In other words, it gives rise to a feeling in which there is no place for self-esteem, and, in many cases, allows the insinuation of critical attitudes to oneself that would not be expressed even by the most severe external critic.

Andy Warhol wasn't immune to this. Even when he was honoured as a great artist and genuine star, he was unable to lighten the load of shyness that had dogged him since adolescence. His embarrassment during evening events in public, which is documented in his biographies, was simply an expression of his pathological and often extreme self-criticism.

However, this phenomenon does not always manifest itself in the same way, although the underlying psychological dynamic is based on identical causes. This is entirely understandable if you consider that the development of every one of us has been subjected to many variables that are capable of generating fear of others, and that fear is to some extent likely to trigger compensatory behaviour and solutions that might not be particularly damaging for our quality of life. Indeed, shyness can become a stimulus for great enterprises and for achieving social status so prestigious as to act as a way of exorcising the concern over a basic defect.

This is what happened to a Member of Parliament who had put his opposition to his shyness to such good use that he had transformed himself into a man of great public standing and of undoubted influence. The crisis came when his wife left him for another man, as she was tired of always coming second to his political activities and of the excessive freedom he allowed himself. But what did that freedom consist of? His dreams tell us more than his actual experiences. The MP had taken the shape of a strange, large and multicoloured bird that had been raised within the confines of an aviary. This time, he realized that the door had been left slightly ajar and he was able to take his chance to fly outside. He was filled with a spasm of pleasure, but this sensation was not to last. The area outside the aviary was crowded with hunters who found him easy prey given his size and visibility. His wife's departure had visibly opened up again the cycle of fear of others, profound anxiety over becoming free and, in spite of his position, the sense of having lived his life in a precarious state of consciousness. Consequently he felt the need to assert himself, in the face of a threatening world, in order to exist. He once again felt dishonourable, in spite of being an 'honourable member' and having for so long put his shyness to good effect. He had done this in a dynamic, even creative manner, but he had imprudently posited his need for love, which was always waiting in the wings, in an inappropriate place. The world of politics is not particularly well-known for its abundance of loving sentiments. Member of Parliament found himself having to deal with the root of his inner experience when he felt that he had left all that behind him. There certainly was nothing pathological in this, but there was an unease that, by suddenly manifesting itself, provoked a state of instability.

Given that it resulted from effective stratagems for keeping shyness under control, this aspect of shyness appears to differ considerably from the clinical variants. On the other hand, whoever experiences this feeling only wants it to be invisible to others, and is therefore willing to pay any price. But attempts to keep it hidden are often like short blankets that cannot fulfil their intended purpose. And then the shyness becomes visible: the greater that visibility, the greater the suffering. The suffering is differentiated and of different intensity. It transforms itself into behavioural characteristics that can be a little clumsy, or it can go on to create genuine psychiatric symptoms that end up seriously compromising relational life and the quality of existence itself.

There follows a classification that starts with the highly populous category of the unsuspected and works its way up by degrees to the more oppressive conditions where pathology takes over.

The Unsuspected

We must have all experienced shyness at some time in our lives – let him who is without shyness cast the first stone! Of course, I am not referring to clearly discernible shyness, but to that sensation of embarrassment and unease to which you need to react in the most vigorous and effective manner you can. As we shall see later, the unsuspected are those who skilfully use many of the strategies for concealing unease, and they often achieve the hoped-for aim of achieving social recognition.

They are usually well-established, creative and productive individuals – among the best that can be expected in our society. They might well, with good reason, be found amongst those hyperthymics we met when discussing temperament. It is not easy to understand immediately whether a person of this kind (perhaps a person whom you are acquainted with, look up to or is in a position over you) achieved his or her status through a series of expedients to deal with shyness, or whether it is just down to an innate personality and way of doing things. The difference between these two possibilities is only in the expenditure of energy and the cost of tension generated by asserting oneself. It is therefore an exquisitely personal matter.

I will discuss some of the stratagems used by the unsuspected to compensate for shyness in the next chapter. I do not wish to criticize them in any way, my intention is merely to consider the cost-benefits of their efforts. It should be remembered that the unsuspected are responding to the need to achieve goals that can create the appearance of dignity and can combat the anxiety created by one's supposed deficiencies. This type of behaviour, as happened with the MP, drives towards the achievement of ambitious projects, under whose cover shyness may not even be visible. There is no doubt that it can reappear, but usually this occurs outside the territory, activity or initiative that acts as a protective barrier. It can manifest itself as the result of a trifle: a question about something personal, an allusion to something intimate, or a possibly unconscious reference to something that has to be kept absolutely secret. In the protected area, on the other hand, everything is kept under control, and it is precisely here that the individual can bolster his or her sense of security. This may be an artificial sense of security, lacking in authenticity if you like, but can create a sense of wellbeing. However that wellbeing may be defective.

This was presumably what Talleyrand felt. His life was devoted to a feverish career struggling up the ladder to a great number of positions: the Bishop of Autun, the governor of the Department of Seine after having abandoned his cassock, Napoleon's foreign minister, the same position for Louis XVIII and also that king's prime minister. This controversial figure was looked on with suspicion and depicted as a cynic and opportunist. His ambitions arose from an account he had opened with his own history, one that was never paid off. Abandoned by his parents at birth and entrusted to a wet-nurse, he grew up with the irrepressible idea of his own fundamental inadequacy, partly because of a nasty trick of fate. When he was only a few months old he fell from a chest of drawers and broke his foot. As his parents neglected to heal the fracture properly, he was crippled for the whole of his life. When he was about fifty years old and an exile in London during a period when he had fallen from grace, and was impoverished and widely criticized, he contravened the self-censorship that forbade any reference to affection and emotion, and spoke clearly of the origins of his own anxieties. This was recalled by Jean Orieux who wrote an essay on him, and the origins of those anxieties were the indifference of his parents and the physical disability that was its direct consequence. Yet he was one of the greatest figures of the late eighteenth and early nineteenth centuries, and history never detected the sense of emptiness, abandonment and failure that accompanied him throughout his life and became the principal incentive for his greatness.

There are many Talleyrands, generally of lower stature, who populate the chronicles of the well-regarded, even in our own times, and they are even more unsuspected than this famous Frenchman whose disability was there for all to see. The idea of their inadequacy is wholly enclosed within their minds and feelings, and constitutes the driving force for their large and small enterprises. This is unless unexpected problems occur of varying degrees of seriousness, as these can trigger shyness on a massive, even dramatic scale. This happened to some of those powerful Italian politicians who were caught up in the corruption scandals of the late eighties. They could not survive the disgrace, shame, collapse in credibility and loss of power, and some even ended up taking their own lives.

Shyness always exposes a sense of uncertainty that at times can paralyse you, but in most cases it encourages great feats. However, even when reputation and credibility have been established by real merit and could now be enjoyed, the need to maintain your position and perhaps improve it by any means can worm its way in. This is shown by the tension and shakiness that accompanies some famous people when they appear in public, precisely because they cannot allow themselves to fail. It is above all their talent that turns them into the 'unsuspected'. Every time, they have to reaffirm their reputation, and the greater that reputation the harder the ordeal they put themselves through. This is why the great French actress Sarah Bernhardt responded to a young colleague who claimed never to have experienced stage fright by saying: 'Darling, you'll experience it as you develop your acting skills.'

Whether they are famous, powerful or ordinary citizens, the unsuspected are those who have put their shyness to greatest use by promoting what they consider to be the best possible invention of themselves. Are they pathological or blameworthy? Certainly not. They could even be held up as exemplary individuals, at least for as long as their efforts do not produce some problem, possibly of a psychosomatic nature.

The Inept

They can provoke compassion, embarrassment, irritation, anger or curiosity, but they are always making a good or bad spectacle of themselves. They are conspicuous, but would never want to be. It is precisely this that makes them awkward, and this is why they wish to humiliate themselves and be given the maximum consideration at the same time. Sometimes they receive tender assistance, but very often they are the butt of cruel jokes. They are caricatured on the screen, as in the characters portrayed by Woody Allen. These inept characters are ridiculed by demonstrating some aspects of their being, but without paying much attention to the inner discomfort they have to struggle with.

They have some particular characteristics, in terms of both their behaviour and their physical attributes. Above all, they are people who have difficulty in getting their needs taken into account and are not able to say no. They are always uncertain about whether or not their opinions are right or relevant, and so they end up not defending them and not arguing for them. At times, it appears that they do not have any real convictions, given that they seem willing to modify them to please the person they are talking to. Reality is somewhat different: when faced with someone who is certain of their arguments, their thinking process becomes paralysed and they are incapable of building the logical connections they previously felt to be well-rehearsed. They find themselves in the same situation as those who think they have learnt their schoolwork well, but when questioned are unable to repeat its content. Once the unhappy encounter is over (and there will be many of them), they are distressed that they were unable to put their own points across, while they also fear that they made a bad impression (and this inevitably aggravates their shyness).

As I have said, they don't know how to say no. The psychiatrist Alexander Lowen emphasizes that

> no acts as a psychological membrane. [...] It prevents the individual from being overcome by external pressures and allows him to discriminate between the demands and the attempts at persuasion to which he is constantly subjected. [...] It defines the boundaries of an individual's ego, just as the physical membrane defines the boundaries of the body. Saying no is an expression of opposition that is the basis for a sense of identity.

But why are the timid unable to say 'no'? Primarily, according to Lowen's concepts, because they do not have a well-developed and well-organized sense of identity. They have doubts over who they really are, over their own worth, over how much they can expect of themselves and over what other people will think of them. This is why they put themselves in a situation that is not going to displease the person they are talking to, by giving assent that is no more than an act of submission, a negation of the free expression of their own will and their own thoughts.

Indeed, this self-negation espouses an attempt to maintain the most harmonious relationship possible with the greatest number of people by pursuing the ideal of pleasing everyone. This is an extremely risky undertaking, given that it always leads to self-negation. By following this route, shy people end up facing irritating and unpleasant situations: losing money because they can't bring themselves to say no to an unreliable friend who has asked for a loan, having to pass time in uncongenial company because they are unable to refuse an invitation, taking on too much work by accepting a colleague's request, waiting longer at a counter because someone has asked to move up the queue, and having to make love when they don't want to. Of course, to avoid all this you would have to put your own needs, rights and desires first, but that would also mean dealing with your own anxieties and fears. The greatest of those fears is that of being criticized and ostracized.

Never saying no is also a way of staying hidden, in order to avoid revealing anything that comes close to one's own secret, as that could mean laying it bare. Saying 'yes' appears to give considerable assurance. It is something that shouldn't have unpleasant ramifications. The agreement will probably be automatic and there will be no need to clarify the meaning of the reply. On the other hand, if the answer were 'no', the other person might then ask why, thus creating a situation in which you would be called upon to say something more about yourself and to reveal something of your own hidden world. This is why shy people are so affirmative. It is their difficulty in expressing preferences, needs and their own opinions to someone else, as this would expose them to a conspicuousness for which they are not ready.

This is partly why the inept appear awkward – they are so accommodating that they are embarrassing and their manner of expression, walking and speaking reveals their emotional difficulties. In other words, they display behaviour that appears inappropriate by being too much or too little. Shyness that is experienced as a state of embarrassment can lead to sudden and rash movements, and for instance this could lead to the individual in question knocking over his glass at a party that he went to with the express intention of creating a good impression. Clearly a banal incident of this kind could generate further anxiety in a shy person, and make that person only wish to be somewhere else, thus compromising the possibility of enjoying the evening.

The inept can feel profound unease when walking in view of others, and they can talk at such speed as to consume all the possible subjects for conversation. However, the real Achilles' heel is the body, which reveals the underlying mood by the way it manifests itself. The inept know that red is a colour that does not suit them, that for them is only troublesome. Yet their neurovegetative system, solicited by the centre that filters stimuli and organizes emotions in the central nervous system, unconsciously acts in such a way that they have to display the colour red in spite of themselves. Erythrophobia, as it has been called since Casper described it in 1846, is one of shyness's faithful companions. It is experienced as a sign of a clumsy and undesirable way of introducing your own face to other people, but it cannot be controlled by the will. It can be triggered in the most diverse circumstances, but it always occurs when under the scrutiny of other people. Any attempt to find a remedy only leads to further embarrassment, unease and the increasing prominence of the phenomenon.

Blushing is usually triggered in situations that provoke fear of one of your own defects being exposed, but can also explode in situations in which the subject is not particularly involved. In the first case, there is a clear link with the shy person's need to keep his own secret well hidden under a set of irreproachable measures that condition his gestures and behaviour. When there is a sensation that the other person is coming too close to that very private area, then shyness colours itself red. In the second case, there is no need for direct allusions to something that must be kept secret, and all that is needed for blushing to be triggered is for the conversation to enter the orbit of one's own fear, even without involving it directly.

Why do we blush? To understand this, we must refer back to the concept of stress, which was described by Hans Selye in 1936 as a 'general syndrome of adjustment'. This is the organism's response to any stimulus exercised on it and, as the psychiatrist Paolo Pancheri has stated, it has the precise adaptive purpose of ensuring the survival of the individual, the group and the species, thus proving itself useful and necessary to life. It is a relatively unspecific reaction. This means that only when faced with dramatic or catastrophic stimuli (an earthquake or a fire) are the ways of reacting similar for all human beings. As the degree of stimulus decreases, each of us will be stimulated in a different manner, and the biological and behavioural responses will be largely specific and individual.

The stress response arises from a fundamental motive: the emotion. This is a subjective experience of an event that must be considered an inner resonance of something that is happening outside. The activation of a particular area of the brain, called the limbic system, triggers a series of psychological, behavioural and somatic reactions that demonstrate that the individual is within the limits of the stimulus for appropriate adaptation (such as, for example, a particularly alert predisposition before entering a given activity), rather than spilling over into disagreeable displays. Blushing is one of these, and follows a path that slips towards what is called the neurovegetative system, whose activity, stimulated by the secretion of particular chemical substances such as adrenaline, can trigger undesirable disorders: the heart rate and breathing become faster and the blood vessels dilate to permit better oxygenation of contracted muscles. Even though this may appear a long process, the stress reaction can occur in an instant: the instant it takes from the unpleasant surprise of feeling that the sensitive cords of your own being are being touched to becoming bright red in the face.

Therefore shy people have a specific response to particular stimuli that they have acquired through events in their personal history, the way those events evolved and the sense of insecurity that they created in the depth of their psychological dimension. This is why red is associated with shame. However, if we examine the origins of this more closely and therefore more charitably, and we bear in mind the biological and psychological processes that accompany stress, we will realize that this particular facial colour is suited to someone in whom emotions flourish in an extraordinary manner. At least they flourish for as long as the shy person in question is not criticized.

Another somatic display of shyness associated with this type of stress reaction is sweaty hands. Sweaty hands, like blushing, are a bad visiting card, because, like the face, they are involved in contact with others. Shaking hands when introducing yourself or greeting someone can be considered the first way of making yourself known, but it is also something that can reveal your own shyness. Some people are not aware that when they put out their hands they are like a wet shammy, and so they don't attribute anything negative to that way of introducing themselves. Others, however, experience a feeling of unease every time their greeting is accompanied by that uncontrollable somatic manifestation. Because of this, there are people who are induced to close themselves up in their own world, wasting their inner talents in the search for an area of security that can even lead to isolation.

Blushing and sweating hands in social situations are not in themselves characteristics of those who can be defined as the 'inept'. However they can manifest themselves when the inept attempt to find a way out from their embarrassment that often amplifies and makes their anxiety and shyness more visible.

The Evaders

We now begin to enter the pathological terrain of shyness, which transforms this sentiment into a symptom. Psychiatry has been very much concerned with this area, and it put forward the first diagnostic category which is defined in the fourth edition of the *Diagnostic and Statistical Manual of Mental Disorders* (generally denoted by the initials DSM-IV) as a 'personality-evasion disorder'. According to this manual, it is 'a pervasive framework of social inhibition, with sentiments of inadequacy and hyper-sensitivity to negative perceptions that appears by early adulthood', which is precisely the stage for organizing an independent life. Without the reassuring protection of domestic routines and familiar surroundings, the evaders find themselves drifting and their shyness insinuates itself into many aspects of their existence, to the point where it restricts their freedom of movement and their emotional freedom. They are trapped in a kind of cage, whose construction they blame on external events without realizing that they are themselves its unconscious and unchallenged architects. They have so disparaged, trampled and rendered invisible their own qualities that they no longer have any compensatory strategy for living amongst others. Hence evaders impose a whole series of restrictions and inhibitions upon themselves.

The DSM-IV also says that they can avoid employment that involves significant interpersonal contact out of fear of being criticized and disapproved of. They are reluctant to enter into relations with other people, unless they are absolutely certain of being accepted and being liked. They are inhibited in intimate relations out of fear of suffering humiliations and being ridiculed. They worry about being criticized and rejected in social situations. They are inhibited in interpersonal encounters because of their feelings of inadequacy. They see themselves as socially inept, unattractive and inferior to others. They are very reluctant to take on personal risks of any kind or undertake any new activity, out of fear of getting themselves into embarrassing situations.

From a strictly psychiatric point of view, at least four of the characteristics described above must be present together in order to be able to diagnose a 'personality-evasion disorder'. But in terms of the hindrance and limitation on an otherwise reasonably happy life, just one of them is enough to set alarm bells ringing. Misanthrope was prey to more than one of them. He was a well-bred and reserved man in his thirties, who told me of his difficulties while asking me not to over-dramatize them. Indeed he had the sensation of exposing himself too much by even talking about his anxiety (we were to discover this in the subsequent sessions). He worked in a bank and came from a family that was not very well-off and in which he learnt to submit himself to rather strict rules. An only child, he had always done well at school, and was very committed to schoolwork in order to please his parents with his good results. Consequently, he neglected friendships, play and pastimes. But it all seemed worthwhile. He passed his university entrance exams, where he read law, but he had to abandon his studies owing to his family's straitened financial circumstances. Having found employment in a bank, he adapted as best he could, in spite of his frustrations at having abandoned his studies. For the first time in his life, it was really no longer possible to avoid living amongst others, in this case his colleagues, for many hours of the day. For Misanthrope, who had carefully selected the few people with whom to have a relationship on the basis of the absolute certainty of being accepted, this became an insufferable trial.

He began to avoid social contact, using every means at his disposal. He never took part in conversations on sport, politics and women with his colleagues, even during informal breaks. He couldn't afford to give his own views for fear of saying something stupid and being made fun of. He carefully avoided any chance meeting by carefully working out adequate measures, such as going to get his coffee from the coffee-maker when there were not likely to be other people around. In the canteen, he did all he could to eat on his own, and when he found company unavoidable, he could only exchange platitudes and make his escape as quickly as possible. Because of this behaviour, he created a desert around him. Even his colleagues seemed to experience, at the very least, a certain embarrassment in his company and communication had become restricted to work matters. However, he had got to know a woman who worked in the securities department at the same branch, but he dared not pursue his desires. His decision to consult me was driven precisely by that desire that he was unable to express and which exposed his whole problem. I confronted him with this, and I made him feel it like an unbearable weight that was suffocating him. He had become so blind that the availability that she was signalling to him was becoming futile, so rooted was his conviction that others would only deceive him.

Misanthrope confronted the persecutory traits of his personality and the anxiety that others would inevitably be hostile. He became better able to distribute the burden that was due to others and the burden that was due to himself and his own psychological dynamic. He managed to understand that he was evading out of fear of being evaded, and he was able to read correctly what that woman was trying to tell him. During the following summer break, he went on holiday with her. This was a change from the previous year when he had spent a fortnight alone in an unfamiliar hotel in Lisbon.

Evaders like Misanthrope are exposed to anxieties that, as we have seen, derive from the invasion during adulthood of the sensation of profound inadequacy that originated in childhood. In particular, they are susceptible to what Balint has called 'philobathism', which, based on the Greek root, means a predilection for deep places and open spaces. 'In the philobath's world', writes the psychoanalyst, 'danger and fear only exist if an object appears that has to be avoided or overcome'. This is why 'the philobathic world is made up of friendly spaces populated by dangerous and unpredictable objects encountered with varying degrees of frequency. The philobath lives in the friendly spaces and carefully avoids risky contacts with the potentially dangerous objects.' While first making it clear that the term 'object' in psychoanalysis means any human entity, it is evident that this particular category of shy people – the 'evaders' or 'philobaths' – experience the need to keep the world at a distance.

We are faced here with a pathological form of social anxiety that originates from an irrepressible shame triggered by the presence of others and by contact with them. The world appears to be populated by extremely severe judges only too ready to carry out their critical task and express disapproval. Only when they feel loved can the evaders come out of their shell and open up. As occurred with Misanthrope, love is a powerful therapy for resolving a large part of the problem. However, they need to get over the obstacle to accepting love, once it has been acknowledged. They need to be willing to open their shell at least a little bit, so that other people can become aware of their existence and their qualities, which the evaders themselves refuse to acknowledge, and can show their feelings.

The evaders also need to be able to read and recognize these feelings. In other words, they need to be willing to let themselves be loved, a quality that is as precious as it is rare amongst this particular group of shy people. Yet they need love more than the air they breathe. But letting oneself be loved is not easy when it is difficult or unusual to love, and when it is impossible to love oneself under the weight of self-disapproval, self-criticism and lack of self-esteem. Evaders can always find excuses, given that they are incapable of entering the game of love or game of forming relationships that is preparatory to it. They will find a thousand justifications for remaining enclosed in their little world. They want to know everything about everything and everyone before relaxing their suspicions over the supposed dangers of an encounter or situation. They end up avoiding promotion at work, because of their fear of new encounters, new life experiences and confrontations with new realities that differ from those that are known and well-established.

They generally become what can only be called dislikeable. They are in the habit of justifying their withdrawal by deprecating what they are being offered. They can never bring themselves to say: 'It is not you or what you are proposing that I dislike. The truth is I am frightened.'

The Phobic

Phobia differs from fear in that it is apparently without motive. You can have fear of fire, a ferocious animal, an earthquake, and other situations that feature something genuinely frightening. Fear is a sentiment that accompanies man on his existential journey. It is a subjective defensive reaction to objective dangers and depends on their gravity. For this reason, it fulfils a protective role throughout life. Phobia, on the other hand, is more insidious and more diverse. It refers to events that appear to lack a motive, but which for some individuals can be terrifying on a dramatic scale. It is an intense, invasive fear that is completely out of proportion to the cause. There is no rational explanation that can justify it, just as there is no way of dealing with it other than avoiding the circumstance and the stimulus that triggers it.

Of all the phobias, the so-called social phobia is one of the most invasive and therefore one of the most debilitating. It is an extreme stage in the path that shyness can take in the development of a 'personality-evasion disorder'. It represents a considerable amplification of the symptoms and behavioural patterns that it can cause. When faced with social phobia, there are no strategies that can save you and no devices for dominating it, apart from isolating yourself and beating a retreat. The psychiatrist Pierre Janet first described it at the beginning of the twentieth century, and it has been the object of particular attention from the Association of American Psychiatrists since 1980.

Today, we need to pay attention to three principal aspects in order to recognize it by the following diagnostic codes:

- pronounced and persistent fear that the subject experiences in social situations with which he or she is unfamiliar and in which he or she fears the disapproval of others;
- the anxiety in the feared situation is felt to be excessive and irrational;
- the unease, anxiety and strategies to avoid potentially threatening situations seriously interfere with a person's normal habits, his or her professional effectiveness, and his or her social relations and activities.

Usually people who ask for help in dealing with this extreme form of shyness are over thirty, even though the age at which this real illness starts is much earlier. They are a great multitude according to the data collected by two American psychiatrists, Stope and Clark, representing between 2 and 4 per cent of the general population with a slight prevalence of women. This means that social phobia takes third place amongst psychiatric disorders, immediately after depression and alcoholism, which are also often associated with it. It is a pathology that manifests itself discreetly, almost in a reserved manner and without any spectacular signs, which are in fact studiously avoided. The majority of people who suffer from it usually realize their need for treatment not so much because of the problem itself, as because of the complications just referred to: darker moods and alcohol abuse.

Drinker was twenty-two years old when I saw him for the first time. Underneath his thick, faded, dark and neglected exterior, he had burnt up every last shred of vitality. Years of fear first and isolation later had transformed a youth full of hopes and plans to become an engineer, into a depressed man on the brink of alcoholism. It was when he was just over twenty that he began to feel an invasive embarrassment when confronted with people he didn't know. He always had something to criticize or reproach himself for. In a short time, that vague and irksome sensation had grown enormously and transformed into a veritable fear of others. He feared their disapproval and saw them as potential critics of his every action. He was so frightened of being ridiculed that he began to avoid nearly all opportunities to meet people. He had to leave university, but having found a job as a secretary in a library, he attempted the path of independence. He was twenty-five when he went to live on his own. After a love affair that lasted four years, his partner left him as a result of the restrictions his fears increasingly imposed on him. From that time, his life was completely restricted to the trip between his workplace and his home, with a few rare exceptions when old friends insisted on meeting up or in order to maintain his infrequent relations with his mother and father. He started to drink and it was then that his parents forced to him to seek treatment.

Drinker suffered from a social phobia that had led him to reduce his own world to an atom, and alcohol had done the rest. It was necessary to use drugs to help to relieve what was frankly a depressed state of mind and only then was it possible to commence psychotherapy. As with many other people who suffer from the same problem, the basic fears were not in themselves enough to constitute sufficient reason to seek out help, in spite of having always been invasive and unbearable. The reason for this neglect of oneself and one's own grave anxieties can be understood if we realize that social phobia should be considered a form of shyness. If we follow up this connection, we come to realize the prevalence, even in the most serious cases, of the attempt to control the problem by various stratagems and to hide that way of feeling about oneself.

All phobic people of this kind are busily engaged in hiding their problem. Rather than acknowledging what could be called a sign of weakness, they put their symptoms and subsequent anxieties under lock and key, a reticence that leads them to isolation. Everything can start with what the French call *trac* (shaking), which occurs when people have to speak in public, sit an exam or confront a new social situation, and then it transforms itself into the complex symptoms just described. But why is this development often so inevitable? Simply because originally the signs of shyness (blushing, shaky voice, sweating and so on) induce the fear that others can detect the embarrassment, anxiety and a particular kind of weakness and this creates a state of alarm when confronted with any event in which there is a risk of this occurring.

It is precisely because of this attempt to mask one's weakness that a character trait, which we call shyness, is transformed into a pathology so serious that it can even lead to a kind of disability.

Taken Unawares

The last link in the evolutionary chain of shyness is the 'panic-attack disorder'. This treacherous phenomenon often comes quite out of the blue, and its repercussions are so dramatic as to involve both the body and the mind. Unlike the case of social phobia, existence is not a training ground, however disagreeable, for dealing with the symptom, partly because the symptom is not usually associated with an event or a situation that represents a real motive for anxiety in the sufferer. Both psyche and body are prey to unbearable ordeals. Terror, a sense of imminent death, dread of losing control of one's own thoughts and actions, and fear of going mad are accompanied by a great variety of physical symptoms, such as breathlessness, palpitations, vertigo, sweating, trembling, hot flushes and cold shivers.

Young Entrepreneur would never have thought of being affected. He was driving his car along the motorway when suddenly he experienced a sense of vertigo and sweating, while his heartbeat inexplicably started to race. He was terrified and thought he was dying. He stopped at an emergency parking place and then managed to continue his journey home, in spite of suffering unbearable tension. His wife took him to the Outpatients at the nearest hospital and he managed to calm down, but his terror of falling prey to these symptoms continued apace. He could only be reassured by being accompanied at all times by someone who gave him confidence and to whom he could talk about his attacks. In short, his freedom was so drastically reduced that it started to create problems at work. When he came to me for help, his diary contained two foreign appointments that were extremely important for his company.

As so often happens, he quickly and almost miraculously responded to a specific drug therapy. He managed to fulfil his commitments, but he had to expose the nature of his original shyness in order to find the key to those symptoms that caught him unawares. The panic attacks, terrifying in themselves, do not provoke anxiety only when they appear. They never last for very long: they sometimes pass within a few minutes and never continue for more than an hour. The most serious problem is caused by the so-called prior anxiety, a state of anxiety that occurs when faced with the likelihood of any circumstance in which the sufferer could fear a return of the symptoms. It is precisely this that causes withdrawal and restrictions on one's own freedom of action. In this pathological state, fear of planning and change insinuates itself into the patient, together with a series of conflicting feelings such as the desire for independence and fear of separation, the need of other people and fear that they are either indifferent or critical, the need to demonstrate one's full worth and worry that one is only demonstrating defects and being ridiculed.

As has been pointed out by the psychiatrist Vittorio Volterra at the conference on 'Where Temperament Becomes Illness' held in Pisa in February 1997, it is unsurprising that those who are most liable to suffer from this disorder are those who as children display inhibition in their behaviour and difficulty in putting themselves forward, or who grew up in families in which one or both of the parents were, in turn, inhibited and had difficulty in putting themselves forward. Agoraphobia, which literally means fear of the market-place, is another possible feature of the panic-attack disorder. This is an anxiety over being in a place where you think there is no help available should it prove necessary, and from which it is not possible to escape. The connection between this symptom and the fear of separation and of being alone has very ancient symbolic roots. In ancient Greece, the market-place or *agorā* was not only the place where business and assemblies took place, the symbol of civil coexistence, but also the context in which events of personal significance occurred in the sight of everyone else. For example, a citizen's departure from his native city was declared in the *agorā*. This was an event that could not take place in secret, but had to unfold before the staring multitude. As in our own times, preparation to leave one's country involved changing money, and the only place to do this was in the middle of the market-place, where the money-changers were to be found. To get there, you had to cross the *agorā*, thus signalling to the public the imminence of your departure from your familiar places, friends, parents and the mother-country that symbolizes the link between the maternal and the paternal, which was to be broken and abandoned.

These ancient examples were followed in the Middle Ages by squares in different parts of a city, each dominated by a single imposing building which could have been a church or a feudal palace, rather than a building representing civil power. In the Renaissance and during the Baroque period, the love of classical grandeur required the presence of monumental churches and palaces. Such elements take us back to the square as a place in which the individual is confronted with grandiose constructions, not just in the monumental sense but also symbolically. It is precisely the symbols of power and higher, dominant and prescriptive bodies that resonate most closely with more personal and private images of the same features, which are embodied by our parents. So the square comes to mean a dominant space that is so imposing that it induces feelings of insignificance, defencelessness and isolation. The role of this space has changed over time, but it still constitutes an area of socialization where you can observe the inner workings of this process, perhaps even without being seen. As in the metaphor of the function of the square, separation, solitude, detachment and being under the eyes of others are the elements that characterize the fear of the square and its significance.

Indeed, agoraphobia does not need an actual *agorā* to manifest itself. A space that resembles it is sufficient. Such a space has its symbolic features and has the power to induce those fears and anxieties that accompany panic attacks. Unlike social phobia, where fear of being at the centre of critical and censorious attentions is dominant, fear of social disapproval takes second place in this phobia. Agoraphobics are in fact hypersensitive to their own internal signals, which make them frightened of losing their minds or of facing the threat of physical collapse. Taken unawares, they have no choice but to isolate themselves in order to avoid coming into contact with the other individuals who populate the threatening *agorā*, given their fear that they can expect no attention or even, if required, help from these people.

Our journey through the pathology of shyness has not only been for descriptive purposes. It demonstrates how, according to the way our psychological dimension is developed and managed, shyness can be a useful accomplice in the effectiveness of the way we live or can lead to the paralysis of all our actions. Its more pathological manifestations are scenarios in which there is no strategy, suggestion or advice to alleviate them. Only psychological and above all psychiatric care can lighten the load. Evaders and particularly the social-phobics and those suffering from a panic-attack disorder with or without agoraphobia can do little else but beat a retreat and increasingly restrict their area of activity. There is no trick that can overcome the problems created by these conditions.

All other shy people, on the other hand, are desperately and systematically seeking out solutions and sleights of hand that can create the illusion of having overcome their shyness or of having brought it under control. Given that the majority do not live locked up in their homes passing the time by identifying their own defects, clearly some strategies are working. They may be dictated by the historical moment and the requirement of social rules and demands. But they may express one of the reactions whereby, in our times, those who feel shy attempt to use a mask, perhaps by toning up their muscles or standing on stilts, rather than attempting to combat the original causes of the sensation. These attempts to overcome shyness are generally costly wastes of energy. Even though they sometimes seem the product of a brilliant imagination and an ingenious and creative construct, they always come with a price tag. In some cases, they can seem to display ability, which has perhaps been learnt from a handbook on how to overcome shyness or through the imitation of some model. However, if you look closely, you realize that they are nothing more than an artificial device: a prosthesis or extension to your true essence that makes you feel less inadequate and more presentable.

Part Two

Life Behind a Mask

3   Ways of Existence

Shyness, even when not in its more extreme pathological forms, can turn living into a veritable minefield. With this burden, which remains undetected by your consciousness precisely because it is in your subconscious, all you can look forward to is a life under the sword of Damocles, under constant threat of difficult moments in which psychological and physical symptoms could make their presence felt. To a greater or lesser extent, such symptoms come unexpectedly. This is why shy people tend to look for different solutions. They make tremendous efforts to disguise themselves and when they go out, they leave their true identity at home. They forge a false passport, but then live in continuous fear of the forgery being unmasked. They fear their own emotions, but cannot avoid the fact that their bodies are unable to live in harmony with their expectations. They become alarmed when the body refuses to cheat and expresses in some way the very thing that they want to keep secret. And yet they still have to live, work, talk, entertain, speak up and go out to supper with their friends.

But who are they? They are what seems most appropriate in a given situation: they are such a circumstantial 'they' that the boundaries between themselves and others begin to blur. It is as though the shy person is appropriated by the people around him, and he loses the sense of his own identity and the dignity of his own opinions and thoughts. Even when these people turn to me for help in overcoming their problems, they find it difficult to talk respectfully about themselves. They exaggerate when describing their faults and they minimize when describing their good points. Clearly the lives of shy people are not easy, even when they come up with strategies for pretending not to be shy. They know what society expects of them and they conform dutifully. But they also know that the price to be paid is very high: it means giving up something that belongs to them, which in itself is neither a good nor a bad thing. It is simply a fact of life, a part of their life, their history and their development, in which they didn't always have a choice. Indeed, it is more often the case that they had to suffer wrongs inflicted by others, which they then transformed into a sense of their own inadequacies.

In the face of this scenario, the results can be varied and almost always reactive and pathological. The shy can try to leap over the fence and equip themselves artificially in what they consider to be their adversary's field of social imperatives (where you have to be ambitious, aggressive, successful, good-looking, slim, muscular and rich). Alternatively they might just give up on everything, falling into depression or those extreme forms of behaviour that, as we have seen, are part of the real pathology of shyness. Hence the only way they can live is to put themselves either above or below the parapet. They are never happy with an intonation of the music that acknowledges their inevitable defects and their equally inevitable qualities, and which can produce a sound much more pleasant than they would have ever imagined.

In other words, the only way they can live is to seek out unnecessary, affected and defensive devices that present another face to the world, one that differs from the one considered intolerable and therefore unpresentable. If we analyse this dimension, we might come across a few surprises and, perhaps, something that touches a nerve.

4   Prostheses

The various categories of prostheses do not only include those made of special metals and synthetic materials. The most numerous, least noticeable and often well-disguised prostheses sometimes go undetected even by the people that wear them, and yet they are essential for keeping up with the demands of the times. They can be defined as stratagems, frameworks, attempts to enrich or steel oneself, manipulation of one's own spontaneous expressiveness, making oneself appear important to compensate for a self-perception of inadequacy, and tormented attempts to make up for feelings of emptiness and failure. These are nothing more than fiction.

Their connotations are not necessarily negative. Indeed, they often meet with the satisfaction of social plaudits, and they often fit in well with the attributes seemingly required for relational life. They can even achieve gratification and can make people feel strong and capable. Sometimes they can be grafted very successfully onto particular projects in a person's life, and sometimes they can make the experience of shyness less daunting and less stark (at least for a while). There are occasions on which they act as a kind of antidepressant or anxiolytic, without the use of any drugs. However there are cases where they are not sufficient, and drugs eventually have to be prescribed. They can be useful for looking in the mirror with an expression of satisfaction or pride, and saying 'I really did well there! I showed them the kind of stuff I'm made of! I should try to always be that way!' Prostheses can undoubtedly be of some use in dealing with situations in the manner that most conforms to what the world appears to want – to what is supposedly expected of us.

These devices take on many forms and respond to many rationales that can appear quite unrelated to shyness. Each therefore deserves particular attention and observation under the microscope, but firstly what is their cost? There is a fixed charge, and prices can vary wildly in relation to the regular and well-documented costs of stress. They can appear inexpensive, especially at the beginning, but the interest rates are very high – those of a loan shark. This wears the shy person down, and damages his relationship with himself and his very ability to continue using the devices in question. Their resonance with the most intimate parts of the personality always leads to a sensation of having little worth, especially when the prosthesis is compared with one's own identity. Some people become overly concerned about this, while others don't seem to notice and close their eyes to the complex apparatus they have constructed to gain prestige and to assert themselves. But they too will have to pay the price of leading a fictitious life. Self-deception is based on the fiction that the apparatus is so well made that it has become the true expression of their being, and the fiction that there is therefore no cost. But then at the first accident along the way, they are suddenly presented with a bill: when the prostheses unexpectedly prove incapable of providing the hoped-for support, thus endangering the status that they apparently helped achieve.

In spite of all their efforts, shy people often fail to use these devices in a natural manner, confirming what François de La Rochefoucauld said: 'Nothing makes being natural more difficult than the desire to appear natural'. In any case, there can be no doubting that all pros-theses are not the same, and given their diversity, they can be classified in different categories. There are conscious and uncon-scious prostheses, just as there are healthy and pathological ones. The conscious ones involve an element of intentionality and fabrica-tion. They are made up of behaviour patterns dictated by deliberate and premeditated examination of situations. Sometimes they are honed over a period of time from exacting experimentation. On other occasions they are the product of impromptu inventions and brain-waves that couldn't have been predicted even a few seconds before they occur.

In other words, they can be either cultivated or spontaneous. The former are the result of a propensity for learning through the use of handbooks or specialist training courses. They are instructions for use on oneself which, in spite of their appealing but shallow presen-tations, do not take into account a person's own particular personality. These are the kind of instructions you can obtain from a seminar on the subject, the ten easy ways to overcome shyness eagerly memorized from a 'teach-yourself' handbook or some doubtful or harsh guru's special advice and directions, rather than from a psychotherapist.

Some people might even get their suggestions from the Internet, where, for example, a certain Terry Heggy offers guidance to shy men who want to be successful with women. Having advertised what she is capable of teaching (how to start a conversation, how to find the woman you are looking for, how to use your own seductive qualities and how to move on from friendship to a romantic situation and sex) and having specified the price (12 dollars and 95 cents plus 3 dollars for postage and packing), she offers a version of her techniques on video. The Internet is a constant source of surprises on this argument, one that I will be taking a closer look at later in the book. There is nothing special, then, about acquired strategies, except the need to devote time to learning how to put them into practice, and very often practice is a great deal more difficult than the theory.

The spontaneous prostheses are based on a kind of creative impulse that shyness sometimes elicits, but usually only sporadically. During a period of particular good humour, you might perhaps manage to act in a relaxed and creative manner. You might then get the impression that you can say and do the right thing at the right time, unexpectedly finding yourself in absolute harmony with your environment, even in creative terms. Evidently, this particular state of grace results from the use of prostheses that are organized through the subconscious. These are used by the great majority of my patients, and they do not consult me necessarily because of the discomforts caused by their prostheses, which cannot be identified by themselves precisely because they are unconscious. They nearly always ask for help because of more general emotional and existential reasons or for specific symptoms.

Womanizer didn't know about his prosthesis, even though he had been using it for some time. He was a lawyer with an excellent reputation in civil law, who was about forty-five years old. When I first met him, he started by excusing himself for being late (he was in fact no more than a couple of minutes late). He was a scrupulous, amenable and somewhat obsessive man who had devoted most of his energies to his profession. Even though he had been married for something like fifteen years, he had never been able to create a genuine climate of intimacy with his wife. He did not trust her completely and this appeared to be mutual. He watered down his affection for her with a large dose of wariness. He came to see me because of insomnia that had been tormenting him for some weeks, but more particularly because of a crisis engendered by the attention and love of a colleague. In truth, Womanizer told me that such situations were not new to him. When he found himself in difficulty or was frightened of not being up to the demands of some particular situation (concerning work, his family or other relationships), the prosthesis came into play. He would turn his attentions to another woman (a secretary, colleague, friend, acquaintance or near-stranger) with the hidden intention of finding whether such attentions would be returned. Following the conquest, his interest in the relationship rapidly disappeared, so his only purpose was to extricate himself as abruptly and quickly as possible. All he wanted to do then was to return to the fold, or rather to the enclosure where he did not feel fulfilled, but nevertheless enjoyed a certain security. He despaired of his own shyness, which had prevented him from having an even more brilliant career. This awareness made him feel a little out of place, in spite of his good reputation, although this was slightly less true at work, where his position provided security. But even this only gave fleeting gratification and left him feeling unfulfilled. Every now and then, he felt the need to find proof of his worth elsewhere, as he could not find it on his own.

Women were excellent mirrors, because they presented him with an image of himself that he desired but never felt was entirely his. Womanizer constructed his own prosthesis from their recognition and his powers of seduction. This conjuring trick had allowed him to deceive himself, but he had been shaken by the most recent relationship, which had brought him to my consulting room. The colleague had really fallen in love with him, and he was unable to say no, partly because he felt driven by gratitude for such special attention. This left him in a state of confusion over the possible choices that faced him. Being a person extremely dependent on his moods and the presence of other people, he was uncertain about himself. In order to choose, he had to follow the path of intimate self-knowledge and free himself from the mirror-role he attributed to other people and the consolation he derived from them. He thus had to confront the feeling of low self-worth that accompanied everything he did. He had to learn to detect the mistaken attribution of causality for events, whereby he considered the positive ones to be the fruit of chance and good luck and the negative ones to be the product of his own errors and lack of ability. He came to understand the illusory significance of his conquests, and most importantly he faced up to the prospect of deciding for himself for the first time. He decided to remain with his wife. The colleague, in fact, proved to be just another of the ways in which he attempted to gain confirmation of his own worth, to feel stronger and more alive, and to deceive himself into feeling liberated from his own shyness. As in the case of Womanizer, subconscious dynamics lead shy people to feel the need to engage subconsciously in behavioural strategies that allow them to lessen or compensate for the feelings of imperfection and inadequacy that torment them.

The prostheses I have just described are without doubt the most widespread and can be considered the typical form. However, they can all have other characteristics. They can in fact be divided into two further categories: the healthy and the pathological. The healthy ones favour an adaptation by following a process that is not only productive and creative but also allows a reasonable degree of self-respect. It is healthy to display the best of yourself, even with slight excess of effort. It is healthy to mask your own shyness by bringing to the fore those qualities that have achieved a certain recognition on previous occasions. It is healthy to use your own cognitive resources, based on your life experiences, in order to innovate your life. Above all, it is healthy not to fear your own shyness, particularly as you are faced with a world that hides behind a mask and is largely populated by shy people. The healthy prostheses usually have limited costs for those who are able to grasp them and play with them at the right time. They are the ones used by the category of the unsuspected to such affect that they can control and manipulate them to help organize their lives.

The pathological prostheses lead into a completely different scenario, where the struggle against one's own shyness produces those symptoms and damaging behavioural patterns we have already examined. They also lead to aggressive, antisocial behaviour and ways of operating that are detrimental to the goal of leading a pleasant life, and can have connotations of dependency and addiction arising from the need to equip oneself through eating disorders, alcohol abuse, drugs or the wilful reliance on medicines. You can generally assess the contribution that shyness makes to operations to disguise it, if you carefully observe people and above all yourself. As I have said, every type of prosthesis has a cost, which can on occasions be very high. In any case, it impoverishes your relationship with yourself, as it alienates you from your true essence and from your qualities, which, already undervalued, tend to wither more and more.

To help with an understanding of behaviour patterns that act as prostheses, I will give some examples in the following paragraphs in order of their consequences: starting with the effective ones, then the negative ones and finally the pathological. Not unsurprisingly, many different ones may appear in the various contexts I refer to. In the same place or circumstance, we don't all behave in the same way, even if we are shy.

Prostheses for Enclosed Spaces

We have just seen how enclosed spaces are not very desirable for many people; they cannot feel completely at ease when they are in them. Particularly if unacquainted people are present, these places can create anxiety and drive the sufferer to avoid them, as in the case of social phobia. This demonstrates that it is not the enclosed space in itself that engenders anxiety, as would be the case with claustrophobia, but concern over the presence of others that drives the sufferer away. Fortunately however, shyness does not always lead to such drastic solutions. Many shy people enter into such situations in similar circumstances by managing to find a device that may be particularly effective. It may be so effective that their shyness passes unnoticed, as in the case of the unsuspected. If, however, we are shrewd observers, it is not difficult to detect how the prostheses are used to deal with particular circumstances. Some are effective, others are innocent, and yet others can be irritating. They can be found in sitting-rooms, bars and workplaces.

Drawing-Room Prostheses

Biologist had asked for an appointment the previous month. On the phone, she said that she wasn't in any particular hurry to see me. All I could remember about her was her pleasant voice, partly because I prefer not to gather information over the telephone line, which often ends up distorting reality. The phone is a good mask for some people, and an unbridgeable gap for others. These two conditions are not so far apart as they might seem, and hence the use of the phone can be a prosthesis in itself.

I was expecting Biologist for her first appointment, and she arrived very punctually that afternoon. She introduced herself with an open smile and was apparently much more self-confident than most patients at their first meeting. She was thirty-two years old, pretty, and during the forty-five minutes of the session she spoke of her work at a laboratory and her relationship with her husband. He was an engineer who increasingly irritated her, even though he was very attentive. She told me at great length of her passion for contemporary painting, of which she displayed her knowledge. She did not say a single word about her reason for coming to see me, although it could be inferred from the smokescreen she put up to any cautious interruption to the relentless flow of her conversation, into which she tried to introduce a few elements of self-irony and mockery of her decision to consult a psychiatrist. When I asked her what I could do for her during the next session, she suddenly became embarrassed and spoke to me of her shyness and unease when meeting new people, especially men, of whom she often expected attention which she never received in the form she desired. She could no longer stand having to extemporize in the company of friends and acquaintances. She was incapable of acting in a manner that did not involve trying to be the most likeable, amusing and most accepted person there. Other people were happy to invite her, but once the evening was over, she could not keep her feelings of loneliness at bay. Yet again she had failed to fulfil her need to be courted, to receive special attention from a man she liked. She also realized, however, that if it did happen, if 'he' did appear and they agreed to meet up for a drink, she would have unfailingly ruined everything.

She never managed to be herself, driven as she was to be amusing and funny, which left no room for any expression of her own femininity. Hence she complained of the husband she no longer desired in the slightest, even though she was unable to take the decision to leave him, because she was convinced that no other man would want her and therefore she would be on her own. We gradually worked on her need to be noticed, while at the same time feeling invisible to others. We worked on her inability to accept her qualities and defects, on the meaning of her behaviour and her drawing-room prostheses that she felt obliged to use but which did not allow others to know her and to know her many qualities, in spite of her shyness. Drawing-room prostheses, as with Biologist, are clearly identifiable in behaviour patterns that tend to prevent action by others. Have you ever found yourself spending an evening at a friend's home and landing up with one of those guests that monopolize the situation from the very beginning with their stories, anecdotes and jokes before you have the chance of getting the slightest bit acquainted with him or her? For a while, you'll have found him amusing and extroverted, but you'll also have had the sensation of excessive invasiveness – the feeling of having bumped into someone unable to find the time or space to really express himself. Such a person is unable to relate appropriately to time and place. At the end of the evening, you will have inevitably felt that you knew nothing about the person who had striven so hard to be noticed. The significance of such behaviour is that the person in question has used his or her prosthesis to its fullest extent. The person is shy and worried about the business of meeting other people and the possibility of them discovering his or her relationship with others. Such a person chooses to avoid direct involvement, which would mean receiving attention but also the danger of revealing something of oneself. The revelation might be minor and perhaps occur through very ordinary circumstances, but it might uncover something that the shy person feels to be a mass of defects that no other person should know about.

Other prostheses can be found in similar informal gatherings, and these can be more tiresome than those of jokes and exuberance. These are used by hypertrophic and narcissistic shy people, who are, as in the previous case, in a grey area between the unsuspected and the inept. These are the people who rattle off their entire curriculum vitae within the first five minutes of meeting you. They summarize what they possess (in order to give you a more detailed account later), and then torment you for the whole of the evening to the sound of 'me, me, me, ...' They are so worried about not being considered by others and disappearing from their view, that they have an irrepressible need to attract the attention and respect of others. They usually achieve exactly the opposite effect. They too relate inappropriately to time and place. But are they really like that under the outer shell of self-aggrandisement and beyond the interminable visiting card that lists their achievements? No one will be any the wiser at the end of a boring evening, and no one is likely to invite them again. And yet behind their prosthesis, hypertrophy and narcissism, there may well be something worth discovering.

Another type of drawing-room prosthesis is the one used by the aggressively argumentative. I am sure most people have been present at an evening of contradiction for the sake of it. There is someone who always has to say the exact opposite to what is generally thought or is thought by the majority of the persons present on questions small and large. Initially, such a person may be welcomed for appearing to animate the discussion, but after a little while, people will realize the threat that he or she poses to the serenity and conviviality of the evening. The person starts to raise his voice and causes the others to alter their tone, transforming the gathering into a kind of brawl. As with the previous groups, aggressive arguers thus achieve the purpose of disguising themselves by a type of behaviour, with the illusion that this prosthesis has prevented anyone else from rising above them. They believe that in this way, they can show that they have their own ideas and subconsciously they feel reassured that they have avoided having to face up to themselves on the dangerous ground of the more intimate self. That is the ground where they have a real sensation of being different from the others, and once they are there, they having nothing more to say – either for or against.

Bar Prostheses

What might be called the traditional prostheses are still with us and are perhaps becoming more prominent. Being traditional, they are typical of the unsuspected. These are based on status symbols and their ostentation. Of course they are symbols of prestige used by those who can afford them. However, they are not necessarily very costly devices, given that there are less strident examples of the phenomenon, which nevertheless retain the same tone. You don't need to display your shiny new Ferrari outside the bar. In some contexts, it is sufficient to have a second-hand Nissan (hopefully not too second-hand), as long as it is shiny and of a striking colour. Mobile phones are a good example of the kind of device that, although now widely used, can occasionally act as a prosthesis in the way it is used. Some arrange for people to call them while they are at the bar, in order to show how much they are in demand, while others make calls to nowhere in order to demonstrate that they are involved in significant projects. Some even call people at the next table simply to have something to do. Mobile phones have not only become prostheses for many young people, but also act as extensions for their parents. Showing off a son with this device that symbolizes ambition can perhaps enhance the image of the family, at least until the next bill comes in.

But there are more homespun and traditional forms of prosthesis. Everyone has come across the regular who no sooner steps across the threshold than he shouts 'The usual please, Mario.' You cannot help noticing that such people can behave in a reasonably relaxed manner in a territory populated by people well-known to them, or they stand on their own, perhaps exchanging a few words with Mario. Why do they give that kind of order? There are two reasons: to be certain of being noticed, albeit from a distance, and to demonstrate at the same time that they are at home and in a safe place where shyness is mitigated by a friendly environment.

There are also bars at the seaside and in ports, where another potentially shy person has moored his splendid yacht. Is this another prosthesis? Maybe, maybe not. Great wealth can be an effective antidote to shyness and a sizeable bank account can be a formidable prosthesis. There are also the mixed prostheses, such as the ones used by Show-Off, a young thirty-two-year-old entrepreneur who was constantly looking for ways to create a sensation. He consulted me precisely about this and a particular aspect of the problem. He was a good-looking and unfailingly well-dressed man who invested (if that is the right word) a great deal of money in enhancing his own image, by constantly changing powerful cars, taking holidays in exclusive resorts, frequenting fashionable restaurants, and so on. While he was putting on these acts to show himself off, one act was beginning to create problems: this was his relationship, or rather non-relationship, with women. He always kept the company of very young and beautiful girls (without exception no older than their early twenties), with whom he enjoyed the game of making them his conquests, and then showing them off to his friends at the bar. Like Don Giovanni, he had collected a long list, but the game was beginning to tire, exhaust and disappoint him. He could no longer see the point. He felt dependent on it, just as he felt dependent on the fact that his provisional 'fiancées' hadn't had many experiences before him, so that he couldn't be subjected to comparisons. He also felt required to perform, including in the sexual sense, in order 'to leave an unforgettable memory' before suddenly making himself scarce. His 'touch-and-run' life was made up of prostheses that suited this objective. He made such a display of himself that nobody really knew him. His shyness had made him lose sight of both himself and other people, who were, however, given an unequivocal role as judges. They had to judge his value, and that value could only be assessed from appearances. In order to get over his dependency, he had to learn to put the verb 'to do' slightly to one side, as it had defined his lifestyle, and he had to learn to conjugate the verb 'to love' in its three declinations: 'to love others', 'to allow yourself to be loved', and 'to love oneself'. After psychotherapy, he was able to visit a bar in a more relaxed manner, perhaps simply to enjoy a drink with his friends. This resulted in enormous savings, in every sense of the word.

Workplace Prostheses

Work is one of those almost inevitable aspects of life, in relation to which shyness can provoke very different attitudes that range from extreme passivity to extreme involvement. A shy person, whatever he resolves to do in his mind, is unable to break free from his total submissiveness in relation to rules, orders and hierarchies. The feelings of confidence and self-esteem are so distant from these people's horizons that, although unhappy with such a hidden role, they are incapable of allowing their inner protest to find its own voice. These are repressed and submissive shy people who run the serious risk of seeing the manifestation of their own impotent need to rebel through psychosomatic symptoms (a duodenal ulcer or arterial hypertension, just to mention two of the most common pathologies). If anything, they have an incentive to create and use prostheses in other contexts outside work, so that they can find some corner of their lives in which they have the illusion of some recognition of their existence. For such shy people, work cannot be a compensatory space, but is more likely to resound like an amplification of their underlying problem. Feeling dissatisfied, they may become arrogant and aggressive towards their colleagues of equal or subordinate rank, but their clumsy outbursts simply prove to be out of place, and create a further risk of their isolation from others.

Shyness may however find another kind of metabolism in the workplace. For many people, working hard, producing and therefore earning are in themselves a special kind of prosthesis. It is not just the desire to make large sums of money that provides a feeling of beneficent but illusory release from shyness. Much more important is the attachment to a role that work allows you to achieve. Hence, promotion, prestige and reputation are all elements that can, at least for a short while, create a sense of artificial but nevertheless seemingly functional security. This can work at least as long as that sense of security remains within an environment where the shy person can be sure that the acquired qualities are considered valuable and therefore held in esteem. 'Hurdles' represent the greatest danger for these individuals, who are partly unsuspected and partly evasive shy people. The hurdles are transitions to circumstances and social situations in which the feeling of security achieved by hard work and merit no longer meets with the same approval.

This is what happened to Successful Entrepreneur, a thirty-six-year-old man who had succeeded in launching his own company almost out of nothing and had devoted all his energies to it, going without free time, significant relationships and lie-ins. His education ended after four rather unsuccessful years at technical college. After having acquainted me with his diffidence and having asked for guarantees of my professional confidentiality, which he did not at all take for granted, he told me of the difficulties that he had had to overcome in his business relationships. However, since he had established his position and his name, it was as if he had swept away his fears and indecisiveness. He felt confident, and started to go about his business without fear of being criticized or ridiculed, as he remembered happening on many occasions as a teenager when he was amongst others of his own age. At that time, he had to deal not only with himself, but also with over-protective parents who would not allow him enough freedom to share experiences with his friends. His secure castle had however suffered an unexpected and distressing blow following an invitation from a childhood friend who had had a reasonably successful career as a journalist and whom he had met by pure chance after many years. Successful Entrepreneur was genuinely pleased to hear him on the phone and to receive his invitation, but his happiness was not able to stand up to the trial he was to go through. During that evening, he soon found himself pushed into the corner. The confidence he thought he had acquired through the position he had achieved at work suddenly dissolved. He found himself amongst educated people, who had degrees and spoke well on subjects he did not feel capable of pronouncing upon or entering into. He felt like a fish out of water, and he felt all the insecurity and shyness he hoped he had overcome come rushing back again.

The incident might have been considered an isolated episode, perhaps one to be avoided in the future. Yet, because of that experience, he felt that he had been driven back into the same dimension he had occupied in adolescence, where he was unable to keep up with his peers. He was so traumatized that, with a rapidity that was as surprising as it was disagreeable, he started to develop a social phobia. He became frightened of other people – all other people to whom he felt inferior (and given his psychological make-up there were a great many of them). Although achieving our objectives is insufficient to feel secure, as in the case of Successful Entrepreneur, our competitive society makes a successful career an increasingly pressing need, particularly for shy people.

'Even though we are distancing ourselves from the extreme pace of the yuppies in the eighties', writes the psychiatrist Willy Pasini in his essay *I tempi del cuore* (*Times of the Heart*), 'we are still surrounded by top managers in a rush, who initially adopt the system's ideology without realizing it, then become increasingly tyrannical over other people's time, and finally show signs of great anxiety'. These signs can lead to the use of psychotropic drugs, heavy drinking or a loss of direction in human relations, including the most intimate ones. This was the case of Programmer, a forty-five-year-old manager who was practically dragged to my consulting room by his wife to deal with inhibition in his sexual desire. She was very frustrated by his repeated 'no, I'm too tired' and 'no, I'm too stressed' by which he replied to her increasingly infrequent and futile requests to make love. Although he was very reserved, reluctant and shy, he took the idea of therapy as a couple seriously, and he involved her in the weekly sessions. He was more obsessive than scrupulous, and took it upon himself to oversee the therapeutic process punctiliously and check that it was carried out in the manner that I instructed. His approach clearly needed changing. During the following meetings, Programmer spoke a lot about his work, his dedication and the energy it absorbed. He talked about his relationships with his colleagues and juniors. He was always concerned about the company's efficiency and proper organization. He used his prosthetic relationship with them to seek out reassurance against his own shyness. In the fear that they might enter even the tiniest part of his territory, he kept them at such a distance that he only addressed them for serious work reasons, and when he got to the office he didn't greet any of his colleagues.

Having clarified his difficulties towards any type of intimate relationship, he decided to change the way he did things. He understood that he did not need to keep everybody at such a distance, and finally made up his mind to greet his colleagues when he arrived at work. It was with some difficulty and embarrassment that he attempted to do this, and on many occasions he only received a cold response. But he no longer thought of returning to his previous isolation, even with his wife. Albeit within the rigid nature of his personality, he found room to forego his need for great distance from other people and the use of the position he had gained in the company as a prosthesis and a mask for his shyness. He also found that his desire returned.

Prostheses for Open Places

The *agorā*, as we have seen, is a place full of symbolic meaning for those who suffer from pathological shyness, particularly agoraphobics. For them, it does not only represent the square or market-place in the strict sense of the word, but is also extended to mean any open and crowded place where they would feel exposed. They are prohibited from squares and open spaces, but in the case of milder forms of shyness, these can be a stimulus for designing prostheses aimed at better adaptations to the situation. This group ranges from those in whom the sentiment is almost invisible to those suffering from pathological behaviour. We will examine them next.

Market-Place Prostheses

The multitude has a role that places the shy in two opposing camps. One is terrifying and cannot be confronted, so it induces the desire to withdraw and escape. The other, which has a more agreeable aspect, constitutes a place of desirable reassurance. It should be said however that, in this second category, the prostheses can trigger behavioural patterns that can turn the bright colours into the dark ones of aggression and violence.

When we are assembled in a square, rather than in a stadium or a crowded public room, two conditions can exist: either our being there has the same purpose and aims as the rest of the crowd with which we share that particular circumstance, or the purpose and aims of the multitude are very different from our own. In other words, either we feel that the situation is populated by friends and people who share our own desires or, more frequently, our own needs, or we feel it is populated by potential enemies or at least censorious people with whom we have little in common spiritually. In the first case, the crowd becomes a kind of blanket that can be wrapped around you to contain your fears and not to create them. Indeed, that kind of crowd can become the means by which you can blunt and diminish your fears, uncertainties and shyness. The important thing is that we feel aware that our motivations for being there are in line with those of the others. In this case, belonging to a mass of people can be an excellent prosthesis for tackling shyness. Such a context might also seem an opportunity for letting ourselves go, for doing things that, even just an hour earlier, we would never have allowed ourselves to do.

Take the example of a tourist village in the holiday season. During the day, you can observe people who stay on their own, in spite of all the stimuli to socialize and live freely. They sunbathe in their own place (which is always the same) and they exchange the obligatory pleasantries with their neighbours before quickly returning to the ritual 'task' of getting a tan or to the book they brought along. The shy, being shut up within themselves, are only capable of coming out of their shells to cautiously and briefly sniff the air. On the other hand, how could they sweep away the habits and fears that constitute the connective tissue of their lives with a single blow? If you observe the same people in the evening, during and after a lively show, they appear to have been transformed. Their bodies are no longer awkward and their expressions are no longer the ones expected of them. They can be seen moving to the rhythm of the latest trend in Latin-American music, and getting up to dance, perhaps a little clumsily, waving their arms above their heads more or less in time with the music. Not long before, these same people were completely withdrawn into themselves. Even their relationship with other people who happen to be around them appears to be different. They laugh, talk and even have drinks in the company of strangers, with whom, however, they have shared that banal but very specific experience. But what has happened? Nothing more than being together in a situation in which everyone shares the same behaviour, which is amusing in a way but would be criticized if it occurred in other circumstances.

Thus a group with the same objective expressly legitimizes what is allowed or what is demanded in a particular situation, on the basis of the implicit authorization that is received from outside and willingly accepted as one's own. All this is protected from censure and disapproval. The group is transformed into an effective prosthesis with no costs attached. It is an excellent antidote for indecisiveness and shyness, and good terrain on which to become part of the unsuspected shy people.

An example of the need to find a social dimension to existence, so often experienced in isolation, can be seen in the New Year's Eve festivities of the kind that take place in New York's Times Square. Squares are transformed into great containers of revelry for thousands of people, many of whom can now allow themselves to come out of their shells and take the opportunity not to feel embarrassed amongst other people.

There are, however, other forms of shared collective experience with a common objective that, although acting as prostheses, do not involve merriment and are anything but a healthy project. For example, there are the groups of individuals who, although generally cowardly and shy when on their own, take over football stadia and the surrounding built-up areas when a match is on. These people are undoubtedly using a pathological type of prosthesis, by which aggressiveness towards others is legitimized by the group. Being fearful, lonely and incapable of constructing authentic relationships, they have to construct other prostheses during the week in which a certain degree of aggression will also dominate, highlighting once again their sense of inner weakness. The use of aggression as an instrument, be it physical or verbal, has now become a widespread method of disguising shyness. Violence in stadia has become interlinked with other forms of physical and verbal aggression that also serve 'to show off your muscles' and assert a sense of dominance. Whether behind the closed doors of private life or in bars and open places, such compensatory behaviour always produces repugnant effects in the struggle against shyness. They are means by which the person who behaves aggressively hopes to gain attention and to assume in some way a leading role. At the same time, that person creates a chasm between himself and the others, a chasm that is threatening.

Interventionist Prostheses

When something is perceived as falling apart or appears to be creaking, you need to take some action. The problem is that shy people fear that things will fall apart or start to creak at every corner. This may result from their fears taking over and becoming extreme, or it may result from causes that have some objective basis. In interventionist prostheses, action is delegated to the outside: to sorcerers who can remodel and beautify, or who deal in sex or the psyche. We could call these 'exogenous' prostheses, but their origin is of an internal, psychological nature. In our review of these, it will be seen how the ups and downs of hopes and disappointments are their most prominent features. Besides, entrusting what cannot be resolved within oneself to external intervention can occasionally be a good or even courageous choice, but it can also be a dangerous investment.

The Myth of Perfection

As with common mortals, even extremely wealthy unsuspected shy people with yachts and Ferraris can find themselves having to deal with their own body. When their commitment to self-realization has subjected them to an excessive amount of stress, they might not only be worried about the symptoms their body displays, but also the degree to which it diverges from the myth of perfection. This can condition the way they behave in relation to others. Before taking on more intimate forms, they may feel it necessary to examine critically their nose, hair, lips, eyelashes or wrinkles. In these cases, aesthetic prostheses, which are useful in numbing (or apparently numbing) the anxiety over not pleasing (and not pleasing oneself), can seem like an extraordinarily effective remedy.

I certainly don't want to generalize, and I am only referring to a group of people who submit themselves to the plastic surgeon's scalpel in order to create a perfect, harmonious and renewed self, through perfection of the body. These people suffer from a minor and benign variant of the so-called Munchausen syndrome or plurisurgery syndrome. Surgical and psychological factors become interwoven in this case, in which the aggressiveness of the surgeon combines with the masochism of those women who submit themselves to an inordinate number of surgical operations and removals. In the case of plastic surgery, there is a less pathological but nevertheless significant variant, where the (possibly slightly masochist) narcissism of those who want a few tucks and reconstructions accomodates the surgeon's business interests.

Lily Burana, a twenty-eight-year-old American former stripper, has devoted a book to this aspect of the question in her new capacity of journalist and writer. In order to study the price of obtaining the perfect body, she went to the trouble of contacting various plastic surgeons for advice and prices for plastic surgery. If you read the results, you soon realize that these prostheses are costly not only from a psychological point of view, but also for their impact on your wallet or purse. Summing up her experience, the author asserted that, 'having consulted five doctors and having obtained the same number of different opinions, not to mention the technical explanations and costs, I find myself lost for words. Is there a qualitative difference between a $3000 liposuction and a $6500 one?'

What is the right price for generally remodelling someone who is still in good condition? According to this study, it varies in the United States from $20,000 to $33,000, although for some people there is no limit for achieving the condition in which they can like themselves. This does not mean that this stuff is only for the rich, but Unconscious Beauty was pretty wealthy. She was thirty-three years old, with existential problems arising from depression and particularly a personality dependent disorder. She had graduated in languages and had worked as a simultaneous interpreter in the past (from the enclosed space of a kiosk) and had travelled abroad twice to perfect her languages, which had proved a tremendous stress. Four years previously, she had married a notary aged forty, and that had been his second marriage. She had never had an easy relationship with men, towards whom she felt an unpleasant sense of hostility together with needy dependency, just as she had with her father, a very controlling and excessively distant man. She had had two relationships that had ended up badly, partly because of her continuous self-doubts that caused her to see potential rivals everywhere and to display excessive and often inappropriate jealousy over her current partner.

In spite of her shyness that inevitably conditioned her during the early approaches, she met her future husband at supper with friends, and she immediately liked him. He also showed an interest in her from the very start, and was struck by her reticence. Besides, she was a beautiful, elegant and well made-up woman, who was perhaps overly careful in her presentation. Following an engagement that lasted little more than a year, they decided the time had come to get married. The Unconscious Beauty wanted a child immediately ('given my age', she said), and the child was born a year after the marriage. Children, too, can be prostheses, when they are used to obtain a new status that is certainly recognized and respected: that of being a mother. This was certainly the case with her, especially as she had to stop work shortly before her marriage in order to please her husband. After a little time, she decided that she wanted another child ('so that Matteo wouldn't be left on his own', while in the meantime Matteo had reached the age of six months). She had a child she called Francesca. After a couple of years in which she devoted all her energies to her role as mother, she started to take stock of herself and she didn't like what she saw. She had never liked herself very much, but the signs of two pregnancies weighed her down like millstones and increased her desire to isolate herself. She compared herself with her husband, with his self-confidence and the gratifications of his professional world. Every now and then, she would compare herself with his ex-wife, and experience a sense of defeat, in spite of evidence to the contrary. She often refused intimacy and sex, not because she didn't desire them, but because she didn't like her own body and feared that, deep down, he did not like it either. In other words, she felt ugly, inadequate and unwanted with a body she just couldn't come to terms with. Moreover, her husband was not as attentive as she would have liked, and as he was not able to make her feel more attractive, she decided to use his money to regain the good looks she had lost. She went to a plastic surgeon. She underwent liposuction on her thighs and had her breasts reshaped. The result was miraculous: she felt a new woman, and her mood improved almost magically. She wanted to visit friends, and she felt she was another person. In some ways, she really was. Those anti-shyness prostheses appeared to have swept away the greyness that psychologically weighed her down and obscured her ability to perceive things correctly. The world returned to its previous colours. In this hypomanic state, she met a busi-nessman of her own age to whom she was immediately attracted. Now that she finally felt sure of being able to please, she excitedly made herself available for transgression. However, following a brief but intense period of secret romantic encounters, he started to make himself difficult to contact, and even refused to answer the telephone. Unconscious Beauty started to brood over what she had done wrong and why he didn't like her. They stopped seeing each other. The remodelled thighs and breasts rapidly became of less interest, and she began to feel a strong sense of guilt over having neglected her children and an intense anger against her husband, a typical man who had not shown enough interest in her after all she had gone through in surgery. She fell into a state of depression and then decided to come to me for therapy in order to cure her shyness, rather than mask it with surgical and behavioural prostheses.

As with this woman, many other personalities, some of them famous, have found that aesthetic prostheses have not lived up to their expectations, and they have understood that you cannot apply face-lifts and liposuction to shyness. Even the most expert plastic surgeon cannot completely satisfy the expectations of those who invest in 'reconstruction' and 'remodelling' in order to be more satisfied with themselves. These specialists should therefore be perceptive enough to assess their customers' motivations (and to be fair, some are), so that they can first establish whether the request for change arises from a healthy narcissism that can be stimulating and encourage happiness or from an attempt to overcome profound dissatisfaction. Meanwhile Dow Corning Corporation, the American company that produces silicon prostheses, has ended up paying out hundreds of millions of dollars to a great number of people for the physical and psychological damage caused by the application of implants to breasts, penises, testicles, chins and noses. Although the joint financial compensation was considerable, in many cases it probably wasn't sufficient to pay off the psychological debt caused by the lack of care and the superficiality of motivational assessments before allowing the surgery to go ahead. There is even a protest campaign against the excessive use of plastic surgery, which was founded by the actress Annamaria Rizzoli and is called the Association of Natural Women. Clearly this is not an initiative aimed at rejecting the prosthetic role of such operations in combating shyness: it simply attempts to appreciate the aesthetic value of being natural. In spite of the criticisms and regrets of some customers, plastic surgery should not be attacked indiscriminately. For our purposes, it is sufficient that those who decide to use it do not think that it can also cure their psychological imperfections, and that surgeons not only assess the physical forms but also the psychological consequences.

The Myth of Power

Precisely because of the origins of shyness in events concerning psychological and sexual development, the genitals can be a particularly significant part of the problem. I am talking of the male genitals with their traditional connotations of power, virility and self-worth. Indeed men are not only worried about the lack of centimetres or the ability to have an erection. Any divergence from supposed normality can cause them alarm. Curvature due to actual pathologies requiring surgery (such as La Peyronie disease) or much less pathological differences in dimensions can all be the cause of anxiety. An oversized penis can in fact be a vehicle for shyness, if it engenders feelings of abnormality. Of course, the greatest problems are created by it

being too small in relation to an assumed norm, which is more associated with the experience of abstinence and also inadequacy. The
trauma of having a small penis has tormented countless males from
their adolescence, when the comparison with the other boys' penises
in school changing-rooms caused them to do everything they could
not to show their insignificant and meagre genitals.

Evidently, not all of them continued to suffer anxiety for the rest
of their lives. Many men, although having a penis of a smallish size,
live with a sense of complete congruity and do not have sexual
problems. Many others, however, suffer a decidedly negative effect,
as though the small size represented their own personal identity
(lacking) and their (psychological) defect. Some even suffer sexual
dysfunction caused by the sense of inferiority in which they are
drowning every time feel they are being to put to the test. 'What will
she think of me, when she realizes I have a small one?' Fear of disappointing and the need to be up to it leads these men to look for
remedies involving both psychological and surgical prostheses.

The operations for lengthening and enlarging the penis that have
been imported from the United States are now becoming more
common in Europe. In America, the *Sunday Times* has called the Los
Angeles surgeon Melvyn Rosenstein the new king of California and
the German magazine *Stern* has written a great deal about him. But
what does he do? He is by profession a lengthener and an enlarger.
He can lengthen a penis by five centimetres and increase its bulk by
50 per cent of its original size. He carries out a dozen or so operations every day and has so far completed about 1500. This is in spite
of the fact that the American Urological Society has found that this
operation is not only unnecessary in many cases, but also has not
been proven to be safe and effective. Yet this is an aspiration that
many men can identify with, based on a psychological mechanism
that comes and goes: shyness and the insignificance of their sexual
dimensions.

This touches the male's ancestral nerves, which relate to what the
Argentinian sexologist Roberto Leon Gindin has called the myth of
the perfect penis. This same aspiration influenced the myths and
rituals along the banks of the Ganges, where mechanical instruments
were used to lengthen what was considered the place of God. Leaving
aside the Ganges, a psychiatrist or psychotherapist would perhaps be
more useful in ridding oneself of the sense of low self-esteem that has
become involved with penis size. However when the choice is
between a lengthy therapy and a short operation to increase the
dramatic effect, the preference often goes to the surgical prosthesis.

Other surgical remedies and businesses have emerged to profit from human shyness. You cannot get an erection because you think you won't be able to please, or because you are frightened of not performing well. Here's the cure. In the worst case, a penile prosthesis involving invasive and destructive surgery which implants an artificial device, generally of a hydraulic type, into the penile corpus cavernosum, permitting an erection at will. Remote control methods are currently being developed and, who knows, we may end up with an extra erection button on TV zappers: if you're not satisfied with the evening's entertainment, you change channel to making love thanks to the prosthesis! A better method is intracavernous injection of prostaglandin Gi, a substance that causes blood to collect in the penile corpus cavernosum, causing an erection. Of course, technology and research are making progress, sometimes giant leaps forward, but will they be able to lessen the suffering of those who in the depths of their being feel so insignificant?

Injections of Self-Confidence and Happy Pills

Other pharmacological substances are used as prostheses in a similar manner to the intracavernous injection, although not always in relation to sexuality. They can be used to obtain feelings of greater ability, vigour or potential to have a favourable impact on the daily demands the world puts on us. The difficulties of living with yourself as you actually are, and with anxiety arising from the often irrational need to display good looks, vigour and therefore authority, lead to the use of stimulants that make up for shyness. What could be better than trying to build a fantastically muscular physique? Thus an increasing number of men follow a fashion that not surprisingly started in the United States. This is the fashion for anabolic steroids, which provide the mirage of a new physical competence, and the hope of being able to carry out exceptional undertakings that sweep away fear of failure. Much is expected of such substances as DHEA, GH and testosterone. They are supposed to give that extra edge in dealing with other people, in making a strong impression and creating a *coup de théâtre*. Who would have thought it – the dwarf has become a giant! What are these three substances? DHEA or dehydroepiandrosterone is the product of the adrenal glands most widely found in blood. The problem is that its concentration in blood, while high during puberty, diminishes with the passing years. It is taken precisely in order to make up for this physiological decline, in the hope of restoring a little youth, even though it does not have significant effects other than slight and temporary improvement in mood and muscle tone. GH or growth hormone is used by body builders to increase muscle mass, with an extremely high cost in health terms, ranging from heart problems to diabetes. Lastly, testosterone is a hormone used more in the hope of greater sexual rather than physical ability. On the whole it is disappointing, although in some cases, it can solicit slightly higher sexual desire.

What are the costs? The financial ones are pretty low. However, the health costs caused by overdoses can be very much higher, particularly for the kidneys, the liver and the prostate gland, which might be subject to cancer. The costs of melatonin are also low. This fashionable drug is not for sale in every European country. Some people believe it to govern sleep patterns, and also to delay the ageing process. This means that it can challenge the insecurities that shyness associates with old age, in youth or at a later stage.

We now come to the question of psychotropic drugs. As I work as a psychiatrist, it is impossible for me to deny their usefulness on a daily basis. They can be used, amongst other things, for curing mood disorders, social phobia and panic attacks. As we shall see, their use can restore the pleasure of life, and is certainly preferable in the initial stages to any other type of psychological therapy. On other occasions, psychotropic drugs are useful for getting through a difficult moment or dealing with an anxiogenous situation. It is not always possible to get in touch with one's own shyness and respect it by respecting yourself. Sometimes, it seems like a curse, a burden so heavy and cumbersome that it has to be eliminated or diminished in whatever way possible. Hence the temptation to deal with the problem in ways that produce the fastest results. This is why anxiolytics and some antidepressants have become the most widely used drugs in the Western World. Following anybody's advice, from their G.P. to their neighbour, local shopkeeper or even something read in a magazine, shy people are on the look-out for the pill that will bring happiness. We should not be surprised that a few years ago a pharmaceutical multinational saw its shares listed on Wall Street going sky-high once its drug called *Bye-Bye Blues* had achieved unprecedented sales.

However, these prostheses only have minimal effects on shy people, and they are certainly not capable of eliminating some moods, which may not in any case need elimination. If they were looked on more benevolently and with greater respect, they might cease to be such a bleak problem.

Technological Prostheses

I have already examined some forms of technological prosthesis, particularly interventionist ones. However, technology can be complicit in withdrawal, isolation and the illusion of having found a peaceful, secure and therefore alluring space, without having to make too much of an effort. It could be argued that the more sophisticated this kind of prosthesis is, the more it restricts responsibility and creativity. You have your doubts? Then sit down at your computer, type in the magic word and enter cyberspace for a few hours – your doubts will soon miraculously fade.

Shyness and the Internet

After an exhausting day in which you have had to make use of possibly more than one prosthesis, finally here you are safely at home with free time and the chance of a little peace and quiet. In truth, the transition has not been entirely automatic, given that shyness can create unease even within your own little nest. For instance, it can hamper the relationship with your partner, causing problems in your relationship and intimacy as a couple. I will examine these private aspects of shyness later in the book. Let us suppose that the return to the domestic hearth finds everything to be as desired or, at least, free from any particular tension. This is an absolute possibility for people living on their own. Tranquillity can be achieved in any number of ways: an evening viewing the television, enjoying intimacy, playing with the children or reading a book. New technology has added another method of relaxation to these traditional ones: the Internet, otherwise known as 'Goodnight everyone. See you tomorrow.' It is in fact a formidable instrument for ending any kind of traditional human communication.

Shy people are amongst the most assiduous visitors to this world. They cannot wait to get into their little computer room, turn on the computer and, with just a few touches of the keyboard and the mouse, enter that seemingly magical world. Here our shy person suddenly transforms himself (or herself) into an adventurer and, as they like to say, starts to surf the reassuring and kaleidoscopic world of the Internet. During this virtual journey, he can throw his shyness overboard, in the confidence guaranteed by total anonymity. He is both isolated and in contact with the world at the same time. If it occurred to him to take an interest in shyness, the problem that troubles him every day, he could obtain a great mass of information. By choosing a site like Alta Vista or Yahoo on the Word Wide Web

ite information technology network) and using the key
ferably entered in English, he could find many thousands
......ms of information, ranging from the clinical description of
shyness, to adverts for centres and clinics to treat it, appeals from shy
people to other shy people organized by some agency, marriage
proposals and telephone numbers for an erotic release in cases where
shyness is of a sexual nature.

The Internet can be used as an occasional pastime or an aid for
your work, but it can in other cases be the cause of an actual
pathology called IAD (Internet Addiction Disorder), which has been
described by the New York psychiatrist Ivan Goldberg. It is a form of
dependency, as in the case of alcohol or drugs, and it arises from the
irrepressible need to turn on the computer and link up to those friends
that in everyday life the sufferer would find impossible to find, with or
without a prosthesis. The identikit of the Internet-Addiction sufferer
is that of a person who devotes increased amounts of time to this
pastime in the expectation of obtaining an increasing satisfaction. The
relationship with this gigantic web of information takes on a life of its
own, and they end up devoting more time than expected, becoming
trapped and unable to make up their minds to leave the net.

People suffering from IAD cannot stop thinking obsessively about
the Internet. They talk about it to everyone and they acquire excessive amounts of material, by buying and reading every kind of
magazine or book dealing with the subject. The most serious
symptom of this previously unheard-of psychiatric syndrome is
neglect of real relational life that leads to withdrawal from encounters with flesh-and-blood fellow human beings. An American
colleague has told me that in order to warn about this and salve their
consciences without much cost, some sites put up a message on the
screen stating: 'Remember to go out of the house.' However, in spite
of these warnings and the awareness of the risks they are running,
Internet-Addiction sufferers, like other addicts, are incapable of
giving it up. The desire to be back in a 'chat-room', a virtual room
where they can meet up with many other people, all sitting in front
of their computer screens, can become an obsession. In that
computer-generated room, they can give free rein to their thoughts,
arguments and interests in a manner they would never dare adopt
with someone they knew. In this new dimension, the protection from
real contact is absolute, given that each person can communicate
with the other through a pseudonym.

There is a complete mix of the familiar and the exotic. It is possible
to speak to the same person on several occasions and to feel a friend-

ship, while it would have been impossible to create such an attachment by meeting the person in real life. You could even talk about your own shyness, as you can be certain of not being found out. This means entrusting a machine and a telephone network with the task of becoming a technological prosthesis that replaces the more common ones. But careful, IAD lurks around the corner, and very many Americans need rehabilitation for this dependency (fortunately for us Europeans, Americans are more advanced than us in this field). What do they have to do? Again the Internet is magnanimous. It provides the required services for this purpose: those afflicted by addiction can link up to virtual centres that operate a little like the self-help groups for alcoholics. The only difference is that the machine that is the cause of their addiction must be used as part of the process of detoxification.

The problem is not so serious in Europe. Use of the Internet is not so widespread as it is in the United States. However, it has become the passion of those who want to develop relationships with others but cannot manage it in real and everyday life. The Internet is used for all manner of appeals and communications through all kinds of channels. With the approach of last year's summer holidays, I decided along with Patrizia Avoledo and Cipriana Dall'Orto, editors of the women's weekly magazine *Donna Moderna*, for which I edit the page on sexual matters, to experiment with a 'forum' (a space where everyone who is connected to the Internet can have their say) on the theme: 'What sexual experiences do you expect from your holidays?' To tell the truth, we were not expecting much of a response, given that most of the people linked to the Internet are men and the magazine's readership is mainly made up of women. To our great surprise, I received a great number of messages, varying from the frankly trivial to those that took the subject very seriously indeed. However they were mainly using that space to find travel companions. They were probably people who would never have put themselves forward in such a direct manner if they were 'face to face' in the real world, but somehow felt free to make their requests through the mediation of this hyper-technological prosthesis. I was not able to check whether any of those messages achieved its purpose, but I think not, given that leaving the world of fiction to re-enter the real world of relations is not an automatic and still less an easy undertaking.

Prostheses for young people

Anxiety, introversion, fear and confusion are all basic emotions with which many young people have to grapple, as they try to find a real meaning for their existence and some glimmer of light by which to make their plans. They may use minor prostheses, such as those for use in the bar, but the results can be dramatic. I will examine several of them, showing the more or less normal behaviour patterns as well as the more pathological, but above all the anxieties that give rise to them and accompany their manifestation.

The Young Today

When talking about prostheses for open spaces, I referred to young people and their violent gatherings. On the other hand, holding them fully responsible would amount to summary justice, if we didn't take into consideration the social and cultural context in which they live and the obligations which they impotently feel they have to meet. As the psychiatrist Vittorino Andreoli argues in his book on youth:

> The social imperative imposed on young people is the achievement of success, which means triumphing over others and continuously bettering their social position. This is success measured in financial terms, with its various masks and therefore an obsession with symbols ... In this way, a clear distinction is made between the successful, the clever and the great on the one hand, and the unsuccessful, the stupid and the insignificant on the other.

But who are the youth of today? They are no longer just teenagers who have to manoeuvre skilfully between psychological and physical changes, and often fail to adapt, generating fears and anxieties. They are also those who have gone through their teenage years and are sliding towards thirty. This is demonstrated by the increasing number of what sociologists call 'long' families, in which parents and children tend to stay together for excessive periods. According to the figures for Italy in 1997, not only did 60 per cent of the unemployed and 84 per cent of students, many having completed their compulsory period but not having sat all their required exams, continue to live with mummy and daddy, but also many people under thirty with well-paid jobs. Hence the under-thirties, who until recently were considered to be adults, now find themselves living a prolonged youth, given that one in three cannot make up their minds to live away from the family (in 1987 they were one in five).

The reasons for this social change are to some extent economic, but to a much greater degree they are an exaggerated use of the family's protective role against life's many difficulties. Young people, in the traditional and current meanings of the term, are increasingly finding themselves bogged down in a period of stagnation with no exciting plans or vitality in their lives. They display a great deal of shyness and unwillingness to enter the real world. They prefer to remain sheltered, by staying put in their parents' house where other people see to their practical needs: cooking, washing, tidying and, above all, taking the responsibilities. How can such young people avoid being shy? It is precisely this framework, which has been constructed by an isolationist society with few prospects, possibly after a history of insufficient warmth and affection, that leads them to give up on life. Hence they look for alternatives to compensate for their emotional and psychological fragility. They do this by means that would be banal or almost rudimentary, if it were not for the high technology on which some prostheses are based, but also with the search for challenges for themselves and others that are of a dramatic and disturbing nature.

Hence the ranks of shy young people are constantly swelling. They have no sense of the future and for them the present is often something empty and uncertain. These characteristics resonate with an emotional and psychological dimension made out of the same elements. The basic defect, that feeling of having unspeakable inadequacies within you and a fear of rejection by others, will then manifest itself in a massive and disturbing manner, giving rise to the feeling of shyness, against which there follows a desperate attempt to find prostheses. It can produce what the journalist Vittorio Zucconi has called the drugs war, 'America's New Vietnam'. 'For America', he says, 'it is a dirty war of joints, lines, syringes and pills that has no frontline and no sense to it, but consumes lives and never ends'. The United States has seen the percentage of youngsters from twelve to seventeen years who use drugs rise from 5.3 to 10.9 per cent between 1992 and 1996. 'The real novelty of the situation depicted by the American statistics', writes Zucconi, 'is that the consumption of soft and hard drugs is not a question of race, wealth, address or schooling. Millionaires, whites, suburbanites and Hollywood stars "shoot themselves up" just as much as poor wretches, blacks, city flotsam and unknown graduates from provincial colleges'. As is well-known, Europe lags behind America in both good things and bad, but even over here the use of chemical additives has become an ugly phenomenon.

When young people go to discotheques, they often feel that they need energy and courage, but they don't know where to get it.

Nothing then can be simpler than smoking a joint or taking an amphetamine, acid or ecstasy tablet. This last one is even called a relational drug, and is capable of facilitating contact with others by suppressing shyness and reducing the burden of formality. Even their idols recommend them. Once the cigarettes of James Dean and Humphrey Bogart were subject to imitation. Then came Kurt Cobain's declarations on Nirvana. More recently, Brian Harvey of the pop group East 17 argued without the slightest hesitation that ecstasy 'makes you better'. This was the opinion of someone who had taken twelve pills at a time without seeing it as at all dangerous, although he backtracked once the storm that blew up, involving the British parliament, began to damage the image of the band he belonged to. Indeed, the damage was so great that he was promptly thrown out.

Drugs are a dangerous form of prosthesis for both physical and mental health. On one occasion I carried out an impromptu consultation and was able to use a personality test (the Minnesota Multiphasic Personality Inventory) on a twenty-one-year-old youth who, in a previous period, had regularly taken ecstasy, amphetamines and acid on Saturday evenings at the discotheque, so that 'he could feel up to it'. For various reasons, he had not been taking any for five months. The results of the test showed an absence of any significant psychiatric pathology. The same test had been carried out on him one year before, when he was using narcotics to the full, and on that occasion, it had clearly shown pathological results indicating a situation of paranoid psychosis, and therefore his psychic faculties had little grasp of reality. Something that had been used to manipulate specific circumstances, by dealing with his feelings of inadequacy and shyness, had actually caused the young man's psychic performance to abandon reality, and engendered indices of drug-induced psychiatric pathology of undoubted gravity.

On the other hand, the group, the crowd and the need for mutual imitation are sources of spurious emotional support for many of today's youth. I have already mentioned football hooligans, but they are not alone. In order to fill the vacuum and replace the boredom, prostheses can be expressed in a cowardly and criminal fashion. There are those who throw rocks from flyovers and motorway bridges. They engage in insane gestures, as though they were playing a game. It is a kind of revival of aggressive childhood games, which are exciting in their own way and can be used to make up for one's invisibility to the world. Naturally these modern barbarians are gratified by the attention given to their exploits by television and the newspapers which, because of their irresponsibility, share some of the blame. For such people, this attention becomes a strange kind of acknowledgement of their 'brave deed' perpetrated through a criminal prosthesis and organized through the anonymity of a group ambush. Of course, the amplification provided by the mass media only broadcasts the 'good idea' of a prosthesis that will resonate with other potentially criminal shy people.

Other dramatic forms involve self-infliction, as in the case of the young men who defied death by playing Russian roulette in the film *The Deer Hunter*, or by hurtling at full speed towards a red traffic light on a motorbike. When the prosthesis gets to the point of extreme risk, this means that the anguish and inner desolation are considerable, so the prospect of death no longer appears to have any reality and its defiance becomes a replacement for the challenges of life for which they can find no reference parameter.

However, youthful prostheses are not always of this negative type. They can be made up of a boldness that only produces minor damage, while still masking the true identity of the person in question. A sense of superiority can be achieved by getting a tattoo or spending hour after hour in the gym building up your muscles, in order to puff up your outward image to make up for feeling deflated inside. You can feel more confident by cynically and sarcastically stressing the defects of others. This is the case of young men who, in a group, insult a girl simply to demonstrate that they are above the world of sentimentality, which is not appropriate for real men, even though they don't really have any idea of what this really means.

Each of these youths is shy in his own way, and they will be in the ranks of tomorrow's men who will have to assert themselves, produce, follow careers and make money. They are all fighting against loneliness and a sense of not belonging, particularly now, when it is increasingly difficult to find any kind of first employment. They are frightened of their present, their future and their potential inability to manage. They are frightened that, without a prosthesis, they really might not be able to get by. They have no idea of what their true qualities are, in a society that appears to demand so many. On the other hand, their role models and what they represent end up conditioning different reactions and behaviour patterns in similar situations.

A couple of years ago, during a fascinating journey to explore Egyptian art and culture, I observed the same poverty amongst the rural populations of the Upper Nile and many of Cairo's inhabitants. Poverty is always poverty, and yet the differences were quite striking. In the countryside along the banks of the Nile, it was acceptable to be poor. It was a condition that could be experienced with great dignity, precisely because there were no pressures to changes one's life, to progress and make one's mark. The poverty of Cairo, however, was something petulant that provoked aggressive and predatory impulses and created a reactive need to assert oneself along with a sense of impotence. There is no room for being poor in the great city, and the price for being so is the exclusion from a life of ostentation and appearances.

Role models, expectations and demands are the principal instigators of prostheses, which vary in their degrees of perniciousness and destructiveness, but are always far too cumbersome. Perhaps the day will come when even the young will be able to experience their shyness serenely, so that the weaknesses typical of a transitional age that is becoming later and later can have their own social value. Then young people could find excellent prostheses in norms and measures that are farsighted and look to their needs, helping them to escape the desolation to which they seem condemned at the moment.

It is difficult to say whether such a day will ever come, but in the meantime they construct and use the prostheses that social models, qualified by subconscious dynamics, put at their disposal. Naturally, they deceive themselves into thinking they have chosen those that have the least cost, without having any idea about the real value of existence.

Young People and their Bodies

A sense of desolation, anguish and loneliness, along with shyness, uncertainty about life, difficulties in the company of others, and a need for attention and love, can lead to other prostheses in young people, that are even more starkly pathological. We have already seen how the body can become the place where the myth of perfection leads to decisions, behaviour patterns and attitudes that are not always helpful for the individual. They are not useful either for overcoming shyness or for achieving the desired external effect, but they were relatively innocuous prostheses. On occasions, an emphasis on benign narcissism can appear healthy. A body that has been beautified can improve a person's mood, at least for as long as the prosthesis, and especially its illusion, can last. However, the myth of a body such as our culture demands can go far beyond this, into an extremely treacherous territory dominated by suffering.

These are cases in which the attempt to compensate for shyness, in its unbearable form involving fear of life and an inability to form gratifying relationships with other people, leads to another disability:

the inability to have a rational relationship with your own body. This inability can take the form of a genuine case of delirium. Here the disease constitutes itself as a prosthesis and a desperate attempt to attract attention. Even when attention is forthcoming, it is never sufficient to appease the feeling of emptiness and desperation. The names of this kind of disease are becoming increasingly well-known, given their frequency amongst the youth of today, particularly girls: anorexia nervosa and bulimia nervosa.

In order to understand the gravity of these disorders, the acute form of shyness that they dramatically attempt to compensate for, and what messages they are trying to express, we have to ask the same question the psychologist Marion Crook asked at the beginning of her book *The Body Image Trap*:

What drives a normal and intelligent young woman to think that the only way to be happy is to be thin? Why do young people want a perfect body, a perfectly thin body? What drives so many young girls to continuous diets and enervating physical exercise? Why do they spend so much time and money trying to be thin? Why does this obsession with being thin lead young and brilliant women to the extremes of anorexia, a condition of starvation, and bulimia, a cycle of gorging and purging?

The replies to these questions were outlined about twenty years ago in the theory developed by Hilde Bruch, one of the leading authorities on this problem. In short, she argued that society's attitude to the body and its value judgements on beauty had created an obsessive attitude over the need to be slim. It is a short step from this to the development of an unrealistic perception of oneself, including one's body. But we can obtain more direct and less theoretical answers from two girls: Marta and Giovanna, just two of the many who have been treated by my colleagues and myself at the Centre for Eating Disorders, of which I am the director and which comes under the national health system.

Marta is a twenty-one-year-old girl. When her parents brought her to me for the first time, she weighed 35 kg, while her height is 170 cm. This means that her body mass index (BMI), measured by dividing her weight by the square of her height in metres, was 12, while normal figures range from 20 to 24.9. Her menstrual cycle had been interrupted for more than a year. She was pale, with an expression that was both angry and frightened, and she listened to her parents with complete detachment. When I asked her to sit down,

Marta showed all her diffidence and told me that she was fine as she was, and didn't want even to hear about putting weight back on. We spoke of everything except her physique, and we did this for a few sessions which she attended on her own.

Marta told me about herself. She had been an exemplary child, who had used all her energies in order to come out first at school, in sport and in relation to her sister, who was two years younger. She had been so busy pursuing these aims that she had never had time to cultivate friendships, except during school and in the volley-ball team. But as soon as those activities ended, she found herself even more on her own. Although she wanted to, she was too frightened to phone a friend for fear that the answer would be that the friend was too busy to see her. Two boys had shown an interest in her, but she didn't trust them. Boys didn't give her any feeling of security or stability. For her, men were like her father and were always away. When she was little, he would always promise to take her out on Sunday, but when it came to the day, he would make some excuse and go out on his own business.

Things had not been going well between the parents. They were always arguing and her mother could no longer stand living with a man who only thought of himself. Marta could not afford to cause further problems, and so she always did her best.

Two years before our meeting, Marta had started a diet. She had not been fat, but wanted to slim a little because she didn't like herself as she was. From that moment, her diet became her companion – a companion that was so demanding that she restricted it until she was practically eating nothing at all. She had achieved her aim of perfection, and she did not want to lose it. She almost deliriously perceived her body as perfect and totally under her control, just as if it was her means of controlling the external world. It was an entirely personal dimension that could not be shared with other people, who she perceived as increasingly distant. Moreover, her parents' attention had suddenly become assiduous. This attention irritated her, because of their interference in her eating habits, but was also something completely new and, in that sense, she welcomed it. What is more, it was as though her parents had discovered a new harmony, and had come closer together. All these miracles were the result of her meagre body and her extreme control over her food intake!

However, the dark side of her world remained. This led to the isolation that protected her from risks and disappointments, but in the end, prevented her from any social contact and, above all, from any emotional life. Apart from sex, this was something that, on the whole, she wanted. Anorexia had become her terrible prosthesis and her method for freeing herself from her shyness and anguish over her lack of worth. It was a kind of insurance policy with a very high premium against the risks of relational life and even of a relationship with herself.

Marta had to follow a long road to overcome her illness, to give up that unproductive struggle and start to run risks with real life by constructing a good relationship with a new body. Indeed, she had to believe in a new idea of the body, that abandoned the delirium of perfection attained through being slim.

Unlike Marta, Giovanna did not have a body that immediately startled you. Besides, maximum reticence was one of her aims. When she came to me, she broke through the barrier of total secrecy that surrounded her illness and its symptoms. A pretty girl of twenty-four with a brilliant c.v. from her university studies at the faculty of medicine, she was suffering from bulimia nervosa. I had spoken of this pathology at a lecture that she attended, and that gave her the courage to come out into the open with someone who could understand her and help her to understand what she was going through. She would unfailingly stuff herself four times a day with enormous quantities of food, and then stick two fingers down her throat to make herself vomit. She told me in a state of considerable anguish that this ghastly but almost sensual ritual had been going on for two years. For a while she had tried to lose weight, but was unable to follow the rigid dietary rules and had discovered this method of eating without getting fat. She felt the need to stuff herself, every time that she felt some problem was getting her down, every time she felt lonely, every time she felt inadequate in the company of others and every time she felt she was failing in her relationship with her boyfriend. She lived away from home for most of the week, but when she returned home to her mother (the parents had separated), the symptom became even more overpowering, although she was always very careful not to be discovered. However, the limited attention her mother paid to her allowed her to get away with it.

She wanted the physique of a top model, but her unstoppable habit certainly prevented her from getting one. She was profoundly troubled. She felt ugly and fat (she weighed 51 kilos and was 169 centimetres tall). She couldn't understand why Giulio continued to stay with her. She felt she did not deserve it and sabotaged their relationship by continuously putting him to the test. They made love very rarely and she did so very aggressively. She demanded a lot, but only managed to give and receive very little. She always hid her shyness by being aggressive and taking the initiative in a very invasive manner, except that afterwards she would feel inadequate, bottle everything up inside herself and vent her feelings of frustration and failure by eating and then vomiting. This secret behaviour had become her prosthesis by which she gave vent to her anger with herself.

Bulimia nervosa was an easy companion. With it Giovanna could decide when to indulge in her pressing and irresistible impulse from which she obtained an immediate and apparent gratification. Afterwards she would lock herself in the bathroom and feel guilty, dirty and vanquished. She felt a nonentity. She also realized that her shyness, depression and difficulty with staying in the company of others, even Giulio, always made her feel a failure. Being very motivated to overcome the problem, Giovanna also managed to find her way out by renouncing the fantastic mirage of the perfection of her body and perfection of herself. She gradually managed to accept her qualities and to appreciate them without shyness. She also managed to accept her defects and to display them without excessive self-criticism. She no longer needed the gorging followed by vomiting. Life started to offer her many other things.

The absolutely illusory myth of the perfection of the body, with its many other associations, can result in experiences similar to those of Marta and Giovanna. This era in which being slim is supposed to signify beauty, this era of pretty models who have to be followed slavishly, is leading to the choice of actual illnesses as prostheses. Unfortunately not everyone finds a way out, as with these two young women.

5   Shyness and Private Relationships

As we have seen, shyness and prostheses are typically expressed in the environment of public relationships. You might think that private relationships would constitute a protective oasis, in which people would find it easier to express themselves and do so more spontaneously. But this is not how things are. Living together as a couple, which is its highest expression, can in fact represent an extremely treacherous reality, in which shyness is not alleviated and, what is more, can even be exacerbated to the point of provoking symptoms.

Here again, the use of prostheses is the order of the day, particularly when the relationship becomes intimate and a sexual encounter becomes imminent. This can happen because of a series of signals and symbols that can be attributed to these experiences and take away their potential to be pleasurable. In this chapter, I will deal with these aspects by explaining the negative influences of shyness on life and sexuality.

However, this does not include those people who, by choice or force of circumstance, do not live as part of a couple. So before we consider the question of couples, we will take a look at 'singles', how they can be affected by shyness and what strategies can be triggered.

Shyness in Single People

Whereas shyness generally leads to isolation and the search for prostheses to escape from this, this is even truer when it comes to single people. Some of them use this status itself as a form of defence. They claim that single is beautiful, almost as though they want to say 'Be careful! No one can enter my territory beyond the boundary that I have imposed.' Whether this condition is the result of a choice or imposed by some unexpected occurrence such as separation or the death of one's partner, the reality is that shyness can constitute a threat to a person's serenity and need to be part of the cycle of life and relationships.

The prostheses used by singles are not particularly different from many of those I have already mentioned. There is, however, a problem that exacerbates them and renders them indispensable: it is the feeling that you have to do things in a hurry, in a kind of race against time. It is as though the passing of time is constantly reducing the possibility of breaking through the wall of loneliness and is putting you in a situation where you feel it as a threat. Thousands of initiatives – or rather businesses – such as groups and agencies, have sprung up around this sense of anguish. They promise to build a bridge between single (or lonely) people and others, perhaps kindred spirits, and occasionally they manage to fulfil this promise. What is needed in these cases? For example, you want to know the best way to become seductive. Well, suddenly here are all these schools of seduction that promise to teach you the infallible rules for making the object of your desires fall at your feet. They teach artifice and the pre-packaged prosthesis, which has nothing to do with real seduction, something that consists of allusions and evasions. Indeed, this type of seduction by numbers could never have anything in common with 'amorous seduction' which the sociologist Jean Baudrillard described in the following terms: 'you are seduced by a woman because she becomes the place where you decide to hide your secret. At that point, she unwittingly holds that which you will never be able to understand.'

But it should be remembered that shy people have this reluctance to let others know about their secret. It is the thing that not even they know, but which they are terribly frightened of. This cause of their shyness is something they could never confess and could never examine. They might require other prostheses, besides the arts of seduction. They might want to improve their conversational skills, to know what to talk about, to attract attention without being ostentatious, and how to be amusing. What is proposed is an endless and excessively repetitive series of strategies and tactical moves to arrive at your desired encounter.

Naturally the appropriate terrain is prepared for you to display and try out the required prosthesis. And this terrain is, of course, the evening, the journey, and the cultural or gastronomic tour devised and organized specifically for singles. These situations can seem a little sad, precisely because they are organized artificially to facilitate encounters, often with excessive promises and therefore excessive expectations, but they are still better than an evening or weekend spent in solitude. For those who are single not by choice but by accident, the need for prostheses can seem impelling and unavoidable. Besides, they are also used in much less difficult and more amenable circumstances. People who live on their own can feel more keenly the need to please others and obtain approval, attention and camaraderie. They can feel the shyness rising to their head, throat and face, and descending over their whole body, so that they end up feeling like a fish out of water. They have a pressing need to return to that element, as though it were their mother's waters in which they were held and cradled during pregnancy without anything being asked of them and without having to give anything back.

In everyday life, which is a much less protected environment, you can and often have to give something: a condescending attitude, a forced smile and the acceptance of a position you find, in all honesty, pretty arguable. The hope is that with these prostheses whose cost is not excessive, you might be able to return to living a relational life, even the most exclusive and desirable relationship of all: that of a couple. Who knows – perhaps with another prosthesis, you could manage to meet and gain the affections of a much-needed kindred spirit. This is always supposing that one exists and that this would help eliminate your shyness. But that is another question.

Shyness and Sexuality

Shyness in love has always been considered a typically feminine prerogative. The endless ranks of female archetypes in literature and stories from our recent or distant past appear to legitimize this reassuring trait of shyness that was required of women before they could fully be considered women. This perception was mainly based on the existence of a hierarchy of sexual roles under male control, which only began to change in the 1960s when the political and social struggles for the liberation and emancipation of women began to bear fruit.

However, history shows us that the shyness required of female historical figures was occasionally and understandably used as a clever front to recover the terrain women had been forced to cede to men. I am not, of course, thinking of women like Lucia, the female protagonist of Manzoni's *The Betrothed*, whose shyness emerges from her whole being in somatic manifestations, such as her blushing over any trifle. It was however the case that maltreated wives, noblewomen and courtesans could use the stereotype of female shyness as a means to gain prestige in a female role, and consequently a more solid social status than they would ever achieve from the conventional channels of the dominant culture.

While this was true of love for a long period, shyness was even more invasive in the case of sex. Moral codes and prohibitions too often imposed modesty, shame, guilt and censure – all variants of shyness – on sexual behaviour, ultimately resulting in dysfunction. These problems were mainly loaded onto women's shoulders, but because of their pervasiveness, they did not fail to influence men as well. Besides, sexuality is such a private terrain, where the individual is touching upon the most intimate recesses of his or her personality, that almost inevitably shy people feel the echoes and effects of their own self-perception. There are many variants, from the more traditional ones such as prudishness about nudity, to other less immediately obvious ones, such as the need to act the playboy, whereby sex becomes necessary for the continuous business of proving yourself in your search for an identity. Sexuality is exposure, sharing and a place where you can lose your head. It is a dimension in which you reveal not only your body, but also your spirit and your soul. It exposes the most hidden roots of your being, including your subconscious.

In sexual encounters, one plus one can end up making three. The sum of the intimate, amorous and erotic experience that the partners engage in produces a creative surplus value. 'Three' signifies putting a child into the world, according to the traditional rules of nature and Judaeo-Christian morality. Another 'three', which has no less impact on the destinies of a couple, is the creation of the shared pleasure of strong feelings, sentiments and affections that can be experienced and exchanged in a free and fluid osmosis.

Sexuality is also a place where – conversely – one plus one can make less than one, and where the identity of one or both of the partners can disintegrate. Instead of being an opportunity for reciprocation and sharing, to achieve a sense of completeness for oneself, the encounter is transformed into an illusory attempt to overcome those feelings of emptiness and inadequacy that drive you and force themselves on you, because they originate from your subconscious. In these conditions, sexuality, no longer a project for pleasure and hope of fulfilment, can become a remorseless threat to people who wish to use it as a means of showing themselves to be something that they are not. It can then lay bare the gaps in your self-awareness. As Willy Pasini explains in his book, *The Quality of Feelings*, one of the non-sexual functions of sexuality is the provision of an identity. 'Who am I? Sexuality is often used to respond to this question. It is, therefore, more at the service of identity than eroticism.' This means that

shy people attach a role to this behaviour that should
of it. It is a function that has little to do with the
people in love should be following in the most plea:
able of activities.

The sexuality of shy people can stop just short ɔ
There are in fact shy people who are very capable at seduction. They
learn the art of using their shyness to attract potential partners into
their web, whose threads are however very fragile. Shy seducers are
content with successful seduction – all they want is to hit the target
and notch up another success. But there is no question of continuing
the relationship any further: this would mean getting so close that
their diffidence would be discovered. Their particular kind of non-
invasiveness demonstrates nothing more than their difficulty in
taking relationships any further, their unwillingness to engage in
something more intense but for them too onerous.

The sexuality of shy people can go beyond the level of pure seductive allusion and transform itself into something that is directly and
even functionally related to one of its specific attributes: the search
for a field in which to excel, as a means to assert oneself and regain
a sense of worth. This is a typically male characteristic. It is found in
those men who would like to use their penis like a keycard to
withdraw a wad of credibility as quickly as possible in order to use it
in times of emergency, when shyness and the inability to be intimate
would leave them with an empty wallet. In other words, shyness and
sex do not go well together when the encounter gets to the point
where it could take on emotional and loving aspects or where it could
have a more exclusively erotic dimension. In such conditions that
require availability and the ability to let oneself go, a space is created
between the partners, that acts as a cushion. This space is occupied
by the same fears that, in other circumstances, drive the shy person
to use a prosthesis. Such devices cannot be usefully employed in
sexual behaviour, excepting those that are specifically designed for it,
but which require the permission, prescription and intervention of a
surgeon or andrologist.

If, for instance, we take the pathology of desire, which today is on
the increase, particularly amongst men, we see that it negates the
possibility of a functional modulation of intimacy and pleasure.
Currently this pathology appears to be spreading on two opposing
fronts: either hypoactivity, whereby the sufferer slips towards a kind of
sensual tranquillity and a timid withdrawal from an area that privi-
leges pleasure and communication, or hyperactivity, that might not
initially seem such a terrible thing, but can create various problems

sely linked to shyness or the need to assert an ability perceived as unreliable. If you examine sexual dependency where it is used like a drug, this behaviour is possibly generated by some chemical substance in the brain, but it certainly also needs confirmation and possession. This imbalance of desire can create serious problems ranging from sexual violence, possibly in the domestic context, to paedophilia, which is perpetrated against those who are increasingly passing from a role in which they were cherished to one in which they are victims.

Why are so many people shy in relation to sex? Why do so many dysfunctions and difficulties arise from sexual encounters? Why is there modesty, shame and censure? Why is there so much absence of sex, so much haste and so much inhibition to arousal and orgasm? Why is it that the majority of my patients spoil their sexuality with shyness? I will give some answers to these questions in the following sections, using not so much theoretical arguments as the accounts of people who have suffered from these problems and have asked for my assistance.

Shame, Modesty and Censure

The above traits are the stages, usually in the same order, that not only accompany but also define shyness in sexual behaviour. Modesty is a typically, though not exclusively, feminine 'virtue'. Shame is a more widespread sentiment that can involve both men and women, almost without distinction, although it can express itself in radically different ways in the two sexes. Its manifestations can, in fact, be more explicit in women, whereas they can be more cryptic in men and, perhaps precisely because of this, they give rise to dysfunctions. Censure is certainly the most widespread of the three. It is the product of education (or rather the wrong kind of education), culture, and norms that may or may not be explicit but in any case penalize sexuality.

Yet the distance between the first and the third stage is absolutely minimal. Close examination shows that they always co-exist and are almost always in the same order. This lesson was eventually understood by Withdrawn Student, who was in the third year of a degree course in engineering. Her curriculum showed excellent academic results. 'If I knew how to prepare for sex in the same way that I prepare for exams, I would probably be a happy girl.' This statement of hers demonstrated her 'methodological' error. She needed to feel prepared and to equip herself with a theoretical baggage that was proof against every possible pitfall. She had never had any difficulty with the technical problems posed by her university courses, but technique is not everything. The great Eduardo De Filippo once said 'We never stop sitting exams', and Withdrawn Student was fully aware of this. Different meanings can be attached to different kinds of exams, just as the role of exam can be attributed to totally inappropriate circumstances. But the student was not able to go easy on herself. She had grown up in an affluent middle-class family, in which the strict rule was that you had to put up a faultless front. She remembered the many problems and tensions that characterized the relationship between the parents, but she also remembered that you were never supposed to 'wash your dirty linen' in public. The young woman had organized her relational life precisely with this concern over 'dirty washing' in mind. She never felt completely free to show her true self, even in reassuring and friendly situations. She always maintained the maximum restraint, while holding in her feelings that resembled shame and invited censure of her own spontaneous and authentic world. It was therefore a lot easier to sit university exams than those on intimacy.

A few months before coming to ask for my help, she met the fellow student who was to become her boyfriend. It was not easy to enter a relationship that quickly, but the two were very attracted to each other. She told me that his expectations of intimacy soon started to make her feel uneasy. She had no desire to have sex. She was not attracted by the idea of an experience that involved their bodies, when she did not feel that she wanted to expose her own. However, driven by a sense of gratitude for the love that the young man expressed for her, she decided to satisfy him. They made love in his student flat – with the lights off, of course. She did not feel any pleasure. Indeed she felt guilty and experienced a deep sense of shame. After that 'first time', she no longer wanted to make love. Her desire seemed to have been permanently extinguished. She had to undergo a lengthy course of psychotherapy, first on her own and then as a couple, with a great deal of help from her boyfriend. Only then did she feel sufficiently autonomous from her past to overcome that kind of sexual phobia.

Before undertaking sexual therapy as a couple, the Withdrawn Student had to confront the origins of her shyness and her subsequent extreme self-control. She had to learn 'to go easy on herself', and therefore to be less critical about her every decision and intention. She was thus able to share some of her doubts and weaknesses with her partner, and to discover gradually that this did not mean rejection and aloofness but, quite the contrary, led to greater emotional harmony. Her sexual shyness receded into the background and no longer invaded her intimacy, even though she still found it easier to deal with the other exams: those set by the university.

Those who, like Withdrawn Student, feel themselves unavoidably dominated by shame and modesty, and who censure their desires, appear to have accepted Francis Bacon's assertion that: 'nakedness is uncomely, as well in mind as body'. Such a view is a product of Puritanism directed more at the mind than any physical dimension. Shy people who extinguish their desire, merely shift to their sexuality something that has gone wrong in their psychological evolution: shamefulness about themselves and hence a modesty about revealing either 'mind or body'.

Erigo, Ergo Sum (I Erect, Therefore I Am)

Throughout history, the myth of power has provided the male world with various benefits. Whether he was dominator, hunter, warrior, or even worker or craftsman, the male has had to conform with performance-appraisal and self-appraisal criteria that, for a long, long time emphasized the absolute need to be the unchallenged prime mover. Times have changed, but the myth lives on with a force that appears to descend from a kind of archetype, as the psychoanalyst Carl Jung would have put it. It is a force that seems to be an innate feature indelibly inscribed in our psychological make-up. Times have changed and the evolution of the dialectic between the sexes has meant that the difference between what had appeared to be part of men's nature and an evolving culture has changed a boast for all men into a hindrance and perhaps even a problem.

The remodelling of social, family and above all psychological relations between men and women has undermined this archetype to the point of creating a new form of male shyness that finds fertile ground in sexual behaviour. Hence, many men can attempt to find through sex a way out of the dilemma that involves will and power on the one hand and the instability of their role on the other. Whereas the illusion of the pace and methods of conquest still being dictated by man 'the hunter' arguably still remains, the prosecution of the amorous and sexual act has not remained unaltered. The insecure man of this new millennium can find himself troubled soon after his conquest by the uncertainty of his own level of enjoyment and his ability to maintain the level of interest of his new companion. It is at this stage, right at the heart of the basic dilemma, that the man might feel a pressing need to provide adequate performances in order not to be driven away, criticized or ridiculed.

Shyness can then take over, and the anxieties over his own worth and worthiness of being loved can cause the man to search periodically for some way to prove that he lives up to the myth. Although violent behaviour is not, unfortunately, the exception, the traditional and most widely-used method is to demonstrate one's worth sexually. However, as we have seen, the body is not always a good accomplice for the mind, especially when encumbered by the urgent need to appear better than you feel. In erotic experiences, the body can actually become the enemy of the mind. It can clash with the expectations of the mind, and express exactly what that mind wishes to keep secret. It can lay bare a person's shyness and insecurity. The man then falls from the pedestal on which he hoped to stand in order to cultivate the illusion of his security. In any case, one of the most common instruments for masking hesitation, fear and insecurity is inevitably the symbol of power, used as the visiting card for one's own virility, the desire to provide so much pleasure as to render you unforgettable to the woman and to lessen the perceived risk of being abandoned.

The desire for a large erection therefore becomes an attempt to obtain a natural prosthesis, a kind of extension to oneself that is not only physical. It is a means to acquire extra value for your partner. Unfortunately however, the penis is a capricious organ. Its mechanisms are fragile and, as the popular saying goes, it does not want to be thought about. Hence, when it is thought about excessively, when it has attention paid to its performance and the expectations become excessive, it can feel obliged to remain timidly unresponsive. The psychological mechanism that causes lack of success has a specific name: performance anxiety. It should perhaps also be said that, according to the American psychiatrist David Barlow, an expert in anxiety disorders, the erection disorder induced by this emotional phenomenon can be seen as an expression of social phobia.

Because of this performance anxiety, Young-Man-with-a-Secret came to me believing that he was impotent, fearing that he would never be a man and anxious that he would never be able get over his sense of shame. This was why he had withdrawn from all social contact for several months. He was only twenty-three and he saw his life as irretrievably fated. While he was confiding in me, he was so tense that the sweat stood out on his forehead. He had not spoken to anyone about his lack of success sexually and revealing his secret created tremendous difficulties, even with a professional. He managed to talk about what had happened.

Some time before he had met a girl in a bar. They exchanged phone numbers and she called him two days later, while he was hesitating over whether he should make contact. Evidently she liked him, but the difficult part was still to come. He felt that she was so beautiful that he would have to be worthy of so much attention. In their early meetings, Young-Man-with-a-Secret tried to discover what she liked and conformed with what he thought were her desires and preferences. After a few days, he suggested that they went to his house to take advantage of the fact that his parents were away for the weekend. Naturally they ended up in the bedroom, but what happened next seemed to break the spell. The young man was prey to an uncontrollable anxiety. He couldn't think of anything except the need to perform well and he was not at all concerned with his own pleasure or experiencing his own positive emotions. It was a disaster, but not so much because of the lack of an erection as for the reactions that followed. 'I don't know what's happening to me. This is the first time it has ever happened.' While she replied, 'Probably I'm the one who can't turn you on' – and so on in this vein. They tried again on a few other occasions, but the erection proved obstinately absent. Every time the subsequent tension gave rise to arguments and bad temper. They split up.

Young-Man-with-a-Secret decided not to risk making a fool of himself again and he allowed his shyness to cut him off from any potential encounter with another woman. He was paralysed by a kind of anxiety that foresaw failure as inevitable, and hence it became inevitable. Shyness had then taken over the entire field: it had manifested itself as a sexual symptom and now invaded his whole relational world and destroyed his social plans.

In spite of the emotional weight of the problem, he managed to break through the paralysis caused by his fears after a few sessions. He informed me of this a few months later. He told me that he had put our meetings to good use and found another girlfriend with whom he made love.

In reality, nothing very much had happened. He had simply allowed himself to widen his circle of acquaintances until a new attraction made itself felt and new plans were formed with another woman. He let himself get to know her, as his feelings began to take form. When the time came for sexual intimacy, he did not cheat or hide his fears. As soon as foreplay commenced he told the girl of his fears of failure and not obtaining an erection. He told her of his anxiety over disappointing her, because he cared so much about her. It was like saying the magic words: the proper formula that does not try to hide a weakness, but expresses both positive feelings and fears at the same time. Young-Man-with-a-Secret managed to declare his shyness and reveal his secret, and so during their lovemaking he was not afflicted by the need to prove himself, nor consequently by the fear of failure.

Performance anxiety can manifest itself through another symptom: premature ejaculation. This dysfunction, resulting from the impossibility of voluntary control of ejaculation, causes sexual intercourse to last a very short time, preventing both partners from experiencing pleasure. She cannot enjoy it, because of its brevity, and neither can he, because he is so worried about resisting the symptom that he cannot heed his own erotic sensations. The mechanisms that trigger this dysfunction can be the same ones that cause a lack of erection. In both cases, it can be an expression of anxiety and shyness that are only differentiated by the stage of sexual response that is impaired: the stage of arousal and the orgasmic stage. Premature ejaculation also highlights one of shyness's crucial problems, that of the bearable level of intimacy.

Shy people have a kind of security valve that closes almost automatically when in very close proximity. Clearly this sexual dysfunction can be perceived as a limiting device that not only cuts short the duration of the sexual relationship but also the space that is to be shared in intimacy. People who do not want to expose themselves will want to widen that space as soon as possible.

Women Too

Pressures over performance do not only affect men. No one really knows what is right and what is wrong in sex, and therefore we all have to construct our own imaginary and hypothetical model that can respond to that unresolved question. However, the fact that there isn't a clearly formed reference framework for sexual relations is a considerable problem for shy people. It is not in fact possible to prepare for an intimate encounter by planning every step, and it is not possible to take control of it as an individual. Making love presupposes an exchange of emotions, sensations and pleasure. Will a shy woman be up to the requirements of sex? Will she be as he expects? Will she do something wrong that will make her appear ridiculous? For someone whose self-esteem is uncertain and who has a desperate need to be wanted, these questions become a real threat to any conscious attempt at spontaneity and conflict with any plan for real intimacy and pleasure. This seems to occur when an approach is first made . This is what the ethologist Helen Fisher calls the 'look of sexual allurement', and consequently something allusive that causes anxiety in shy people.

Fear of this look is amplified as proximity increases. In the bedroom, where modesty and shame can become dominant, it can be difficult for the woman to stand the man looking at her, even if he does so with admiration. Some people solve the problem simply by switching off the light. But women like Masked Woman find more complex solutions loaded with symbolism. She had been married for five years and sex had always been a big problem for her. Inhibition, modesty and fear had paralysed any hint of desire. However, she was the dominant one in the couple and she made up for her crushingly low self-esteem by working extremely hard. Sexual relations with her husband were therefore limited, and nearly always resulted from his insistence. She felt ashamed of being naked, partly because she didn't like her body, and she felt uneasy about the expression of pleasure on her husband's face. This is why she sought and found a solution that put her more at ease: before making love, she had him blindfold her so that she was isolated from everything that was going on. She did not do it to be more intimate with herself, but in order to hide herself. This was the same illusion as that of the child who thinks it cannot be seen if it covers its eyes with a small screen, in spite of the inadequacy of its hiding place.

Masked Woman was in exactly the same dimension of self-deception. She feared the intimacy of sexual intercourse, but above all she feared the possibility that someone's eyes should go where hers wouldn't dare to follow. This negation of the sexual act made it impossible to attain pleasure, and she timidly contented herself with the small and illusory assurance provided by covering her eyes. It took a long time to find a way of living more in the open, and she had to revisit many of the dynamics going right back to her infancy that had determined her current anxieties. Before confronting the sexual problem, she had to deal with many other aspects of her life in which shyness prevented her from seeing things clearly and revealing herself without apprehension. She finally had to learn to observe herself carefully and to look at the world around her, which, thanks to her qualities, could now become beautiful. Gradually she became increasingly aware that she could live with her shyness without feeling weak and defenceless. She began to perceive that shyness has some qualities.

You don't have to want darkness to hide your lovemaking for shyness to cause disappointments in the preparation for pleasure. Sometimes shy women are more concerned about possible disappointments for their partner than for themselves. In such circumstances, concerns about performing in the required manner lead to an expectation of pleasure that never comes, and, as in the case of men, this means experiencing a performance anxiety. Clearly, the connotations are somewhat different in terms of the sexual function, but wholly similar in terms of the prospect of achieving pleasure. This particular kind of anxiety becomes so intrusive that it prevents a woman from being aware of herself and attending to her own sexual wellbeing, while she attentively awaits the orgasm that never comes precisely because of the excessive attention. Hence, the feeling of incompleteness and inadequacy finds another reason to further consolidate itself.

It is not uncommon for women who come for treatment for the absence of orgasms during sexual intercourse to be interested as much in alleviating their sense of incompleteness caused by this absence as in achieving its pleasure. Not being fully proficient in sexual experience and not feeling yourself to be so creates a sense of consternation, and confronts you with a situation in which prostheses not only do not function but are nowhere to be found.

Another reason for being unable to reach an orgasm is the presence of what I have called elsewhere the 'Little Red Riding Hood syndrome'. This is a condition, which starts as a tendency and becomes a habit, involving a certain degree of aggressiveness in order to overcome a sense of being dominated. In this case, the meaning of the folk tale should be inverted as follows: 'When Little Red Riding Hood goes down to the wood, big bad wolves would be well-advised to steer clear or they will be in for a nasty surprise.' This means that such women are drawn into difficult relationships, as though they constitute a challenge, in order to confront rather than meet someone they look on as a wolf, and to symbolically play out his defeat. They leave nothing to chance, adopting defensive and attacking roles at the same time. Thus they cannot concede the emotional space for real involvement, so great is their fear of being subdued. They are so wrapped up in safeguarding their intimacy that they end up withdrawing into themselves, not to cultivate their growing pleasure and let it develop, but to demand maximum performance of themselves, which often does not coincide with maximum pleasure.

The lack of an orgasm is not the only sign of shyness. It can be translated into a sexual symptom and dysfunction that could be considered an extreme example of all the psychological ingredients that shyness imposes on the body. It is called vaginismus, and is a pathology caused by the tight contraction of the muscles situated at the entrance to the vagina, which impedes penetration. It constitutes a form of shyness in relation to one's own body and knowledge of one's most intimate parts that is more extreme than wariness about revealing oneself to one's partner.

It was a genuine phobia in the case of Sleeping Beauty, as with the majority of women who suffer from it. For this young woman who spoke of her sexuality with a serenity that amounted to detachment, the dysfunction had roots that went well back. At the age of ten she was sexually molested by an uncle, and she felt so guilty that she kept that secret to herself. Even the adult rationalism with which she retold that ugly experience was not enough to free her of that feeling. Up to the age of twenty-four, she had only had platonic relationships and these had all come to an end, partly because she hadn't allowed anything sexual. A year before she came to see me, she had met a man slightly older than her and fallen in love with him. Overcoming understandable difficulties, she decided to make love to him and then came up against this symptom. It was not difficult to solve this with a short sexual therapy as a couple, as occurs in practically all such cases. It proved more difficult to help her find greater harmony with her body and herself, to free herself from at least some of the burden of her shyness that limited her ability to express feelings and emotions. That limitation did not only affect her sexual relations.

Who Am I?

Shyness and its variants do not always lead to dysfunctions that fall into the diagnostic categories of sexology. Its influence on the sphere of sexual activity can also have effects of a purely psychological nature, in which the body does not appear to be directly involved. These more subtle and more invasive questions are currently affecting an increasing number of young people.

They are disorders concerning sexual identity and doubts relating not only to the already complex question of whether one is homosexual, but above all the difficult definition of one's own identity. This is one of the manifestations of youthful anxiety that can be accompanied by other pathologies (we have already seen, for example, what happens with anorexia), but it can manifest itself as a relatively isolated problem.

A product of psychosexual development in a familial environment lacking in warmth and attention, and of the revolution in parental roles, sexual identity disorder can take on features that come close to delirium. This was the case of Obsessive Youth, who turned to me with a psychiatric problem: an obsessive-compulsive disorder. Because of this condition, he found himself constantly washing his hands throughout the day, every time he touched something that suggested the idea of dirt. Many hours of the day were taken up by this and other control rituals, which although unwanted proved inescapable, creating many difficulties in keeping up with his university studies. He was in his second year at the Faculty of Business and Economics, a choice his father had strongly advocated and he had accepted almost passively. I prescribed a treatment with psychotropic drugs during his course of psychotherapy, and he told me of his 'secret'. In spite of not having any social relations as a result of the symptoms of control in compliance with a form of shyness that increasingly resembled social phobia, he had on several occasions felt attracted to men of his own age. He experienced these sensations with increasing anxiety, because he rejected the idea of being a 'queer'. He perceived the world of homosexuality as something alien and did not feel that he could belong to it. Yet the attraction was really strong. So he built another barrier to these impulses.

He developed the particular sensation that inside he was not a man but a woman, but the sensation did not push him into a transsexual dimension. Indeed, he did not want to transform himself into a woman physically. He was happy being a man. The 'feminine' part was in his brain. He had constructed a psychological device that protected him from any risk of either homosexual or heterosexual encounters. Obsessive Youth desired a relationship with a man who could love him like a woman. In other words, he had created the largest possible barrier between himself and others, between his own emotions and affections, and those of anyone else who could attract his attention. Because of all this, he had ended up not knowing who he was any more. He only knew that he did not feel worthy of meeting anyone else and forming a relationship with them. During the course of psychotherapy, he had to go through a phase of depression in order to reacquire a reasonable relationship with reality. His reality had been made up of fears in which control, hesitations and shyness had taken over the entire field.

The case of Obsessive Youth was certainly a rather exceptional one, in which the extent of the sexual identity disorder went beyond that of a more typical example of the problem. However it did have some basic features in common with many other cases. Indeed, for many of today's youth, the deficiency of affection and the precariousness of values for guidance are combined with the impossibility of identifying with a parental model that has a clearly defined educative role. This factor can amplify uncertainty about one's being, potentials, plans and self-awareness, including one's own sexual identity.

6 Shyness and Life as a Couple

As we have seen, many couples constitute fragile models for their children, and many also suffer from an intrinsic fragility that mainly derives from aspects of the personalities and temperaments of each partner. These are couples in which the essence of one partner resonates negatively with the shyness of the other. This can result in communication difficulties, censure, relational voids, and impediments to the expression of their own feelings, which are all causes of unhappiness in the couple's life together. Desires are important in relational life, but needs are even more important. Every one of us is needy to a greater or lesser extent. We need warmth, love, affection, and understanding. We need to be listened to and to feel that we exist for the other. These sentiments are to be found in the whole of humanity, but they are often treated as though they were weaknesses that, as such, should never be shown for fear of reproach or loss of credibility.

This is why it seems that needs can only be expressed in secure territories, guaranteed by universal codes and ancient practices. This is true of the active phases of courtship, when it is considered possible and permissible to reveal yourself, unless hampered by shyness. However, during this moment of encounter between two people, there may be comfort to be found in the dependable esteem displayed by the other person that can, at least temporarily, strengthen your self-esteem. Someone in love can say without too many fears: 'I need you, I want to be with you, I need your caresses, I need your kisses, I need your love.' In such a magic moment, these sentiments do not appear shabby or outrageous. Such expressions are part of the rules of the game, and demonstrate the significance attached to it by the person who engages in its intensity and beauty.

But when the courtship phase ends, the ability to communicate these needs can also diminish to the point where shyness can impede the expression of powerful desires. You can then be seized by modesty or shame over feeling that particular form of neediness, just as censure can prevent you from displaying them to your partner. This does not mean that these couples are in a crisis situation. It can occur in well-established couples that are apparently functioning without any tensions. Thus diffidence and shyness about rekindling demands for needs to be satisfied can, as Honoré de Balzac said, cause marriage to be in constant battle against the monster that devours everything. Habit is the monster – that is to say the bad habit of taking things for granted, including the rule on inhibition and silence.

Shy people can consequently feel even more anxious if they have to control the way they feel in the presence of their partner, so they are impelled to use some form of prosthesis, particularly in shared social situations. Indeed, shy people can be frightened of openly showing their weaknesses to someone with whom they share their lives, because they think that this might cause the other person to have a lower opinion of them. Equally it may be impossible to speak of the difficulties encountered outside the family, such as failures, obstacles, criticisms or a senior colleague's oppressive behaviour that can cause anxiety and frustration, again because of the fear of losing esteem. Shyness in communication between partners can form a void that serves to maintain an illusory self-image, but is certainly not conducive to a lively relationship together. In order to establish a little more clearly whether there is any risk of this, it would be useful to compare oneself with the following four psychological categories. They do not define actual character traits, but rather attitudes that are adopted in life as a couple.

1. Passive-dependants. The people in this group are more saintly than heroic. They cannot do without the dependency on their partner. They almost defend that dependency, and through it try to acquire merit and esteem in their partner's eyes. They are men and women who devote themselves punctiliously to their partner.

He fulfils his familial and social duties in an impeccable manner, and never indulges in projects of self-assertion. She unswervingly does all she can to fulfil her traditional feminine role of good mother and good wife. In other words, she is the quintessential materfamilias. Besides, haven't centuries of history told us that this is how things should be done?

You can tell if you belong to this category from the subordinate psychological condition in which you put yourself in relation to your partner, in the patient expectation that your own needs will be understood intuitively and then satisfied. You can also tell by judging how often you fail to listen to your own needs to act freely and how little opposition you put up to those displayed and acted upon by your partner. Passive-dependants mainly use prostheses of a domestic nature in the search for approval through faultless behaviour. Their shyness leads them to make a series of sacrifices and they have a latent aggressiveness that can be detected by the expert eye.

2. Active-dependants. They are busy and reliable. They believe in the partnership and its certainties more than an inattentive observer would think. They need security and a reliable source of affection, on which they are highly dependent in order to engage in some timid exploit.

They suffer from considerable inhibition in their emotional life, as this involves the affections on which their security is based. This is why their active approach is the basis of the prosthesis, through which they defend themselves from the fear of not receiving the recognition they need. Keeping busy thus becomes functional in receiving approval, consideration and love. They attempt to achieve so much esteem through their activities as to be able to play the dominant role in the couple, but this usually turns out to be illusory. They do this not out of a real sense of vocation, but because of their need to control the situation. Their uncertain self-esteem leads them to see adversaries around every corner, and they can even have a paranoid view of life as a couple.

Because of this, they tend to construct a protective barrier around themselves, and this restricts the other person's needs for space and freedom, as well as their own. The link between activity on the one hand and insecurity and shyness on the other is not always easy to detect, but unmistakable signs are his tendency to present himself too much as the active and 'penetrating' male, and her tendency to act the heroine in all aspects of life.

3. Passive-independents. They have a genuinely non-stick exterior. They can look after themselves and often do so to the detriment of their partner's needs, even though they sometimes appear to be in the subordinate role in the relationship. The truth is that they allow things to take a certain course as long as it means a quiet life. They rarely enter into conflict and prefer to leave the partner to make any proposals, without getting too involved themselves. Remonstrance and criticism pass passive-independents by, like water off a duck's back. They are always ready to minimize things and to find alternatives when things get difficult for the couple.

Of course, they experience their own emotions. Indeed they feel them very strongly, and this is why they tend to maintain and defend their independence, so that they can give their emotions a free rein and not come into too close a contact with them. A relationship with another person is a nest in which they put a great deal of trust, which they certainly need but to which they are incapable of making any significant or creative contribution. They can suffer from an inhibited sexual desire, given that sex also requires taking an initiative. For both men and women, the demand for independence and the stubborn search for alternative free spaces outside the couple is nothing more than a prosthesis and an attempt to avoid a real relationship with their partner. Above all they don't want a relationship with themselves and with that personal dimension that they passively feel almost obliged to keep well hidden.

4. Active-independents. They are courageous and receptive. They can contribute real creativity to a relationship. They are emotionally free, so that they can fully experience the relationship as a couple without fear of losing their partner when he or she leaves to cultivate a personal space and freedom. This category appears less shy and more self-aware in relation to the partner. Indeed, being active allows them also to express needs and desires without fear of being flattened by any frustrations. However, they have a need to maintain a certain degree of control over the relationship and therefore have a tendency to breach of trust.

If they find someone willing to share their outlook, they can make extraordinary, sparkling and never-tiresome companions. If, however, they end up with someone who tries to restrict them, they may prove incapable of mediating with his or her demands.

Whether they are men or women, they are compelling and decisive. They make the couple function, and they model it to their propensities and requirements. They can be a little superficial in the world of emotions and affection. Busy as they are, they are not able to find time to dwell on the aspects of life that are less pragmatic, more indeterminate and perhaps more romantic. Active-independents are definitely not advisable for those who want a more intimate relationship.

A Few Mixtures

Direct experience, much more than any theory, teaches us that living together places the psychological traits of the two partners under an implicit or explicit need for continual comparison. This can result in useful adjustments, but also in firm resistance. However, the psychological make-up that each partner brings to the relationship cannot go unobserved. Indeed this is the premise on which the health or pathology of the couple is built. The four categories we have just seen do not therefore have much significance in themselves, and it is the various permutations in which they can mix together that matter. In many cases, the shyness of one partner can solicit loving acceptance from the other, but also misunderstandings, resentments, difficulties in communication and expectations that are not met. In the latter cases, it is not uncommon for states of discomfort to turn into genuine pathologies that can compromise the quality of life of both partners.

Failed Athlete was a passive-dependant. He was thirty years old and very fit. He had devoted himself to basketball, but had not achieved what was expected of him, because of his lack of competitiveness. Hence he diverted his energies to land-surveying, in which he had originally trained. He had been married for two years to a woman who was indisputably an active-independent. She loved him, but her manner and way of life became a continuous challenge to him, and he became increasingly insecure, reserved and shy. He consulted me because her sexual desire had been gradually diminishing, and Failed Athlete felt his fears and insecurity growing. His active-independent wife complained about having to take all the decisions, including those he delegated to her, although deep down she did not mind this at all. She grumbled that he did not support her in her decisions, and never took an active or critical part. He justified himself by emphasizing her qualities, which were the reason why he trusted her. She wouldn't make a mistake, or in any case, she would manage much better than he ever would. This was in a way an act of love and recognition, but it could not produce any good effects.

In truth, Failed Athlete stood on the sidelines not so much for those noble reasons, as because of his tremendous fear of failure. He preferred her to take control of their lives together rather than risk disapproval. On the other hand, he had grown up in a family that had never given him much support in developing self-confidence. He had even chosen sport to prove himself better than he felt. But even there, he was penalized by his shyness. At a session on his own, Failed Athlete revealed that he was going through a difficult period financially, but he didn't feel he could tell his wife with whom he continued to maintain the same lifestyle that was certainly not conducive to saving. On the other hand, she was accustomed to living like that, as she had come from a much more affluent family than he had. For this reason, he had not been putting up any opposition to the fact that she was widening the horizons of her personal life and that, apart from her teaching, she was cultivating interests and friendships that often took her out of the house. He hoped that she would be grateful to him for this, but he also started to fear that she might have fallen in love with someone else.

In reality, his active-independent wife wasn't even thinking about an affair and was very attached to him, even if his inertia seemed like a lack of authenticity to her. She was right, and that was why we spent a lot of time working on their communication difficulties and his reluctance to express his emotions and problems. In the end, he managed to talk to her about his financial worries and problems at work. The woman, who was so different from him and whom he considered such an inflexible critic, proved to be very understanding and even helpful. Their characters were very different, but they had discovered a reason for becoming accomplices, and once the shy Failed Athlete was in the open, he became even more desirable to her.

This first mixture of psychological categories has given us some idea of the problems that can arise, but also of the positive outcomes that can occur. We will find similar features in the next two examples. Naturally, positive outcomes are certainly not the rule in such cases, but I prefer to dwell on an optimistic approach, which fortunately my therapeutic experience allows me to develop. This was also the case of Teflon Man, who alarmed his wife for very different reasons from those of Failed Athlete. As a passive-independent, he left to her, an active-dependant, the task of managing their relational life. He was nearly forty and a bank official. He had developed a knack for speedily extricating himself from situations that might be too demanding or risk exposing him. For this reason, he had committed himself to a series of activities outside work, in order to avoid the risk of coming into close contact with people. This way of doing things, which had provided many guarantees, had begun to cause a sexual symptom that was creating not inconsiderable problems in their conjugal relationship. He was suffering from premature ejaculation, by which he obstinately managed to protect himself from any intimate involvement. His wife was all the more distressed because, while used to being in control, she found herself in circumstances where she was always missing out and could never do anything to solve the problem. Although she was an active-dependant, and very committed to running her business, from which she obtained undoubted pleasure, fulfilment and economic independence, she needed intimacy and warmth from her husband at home. She was accustomed to his absences due to various commitments, and she no longer cared very much. Ultimately, she held the reins of their relationship. That symptom, however, had questioned many things, including his character and his detached approach to their life as a couple.

As sometimes occurs, the dysfunction turned out to be beneficial. It allowed them to confront the reasons for his reticence and his need to keep his feelings at a distance in order not to reveal them. Teflon Man began to understand his insecurity and shyness more clearly, and how his many activities were nothing more than prostheses. He managed to make his lovemaking last. So while he gained greater control over his ejaculation in sex, he also managed to renounce a degree of self-control in his emotional relationship. This had been why on too many occasions, nothing that could have led to conflict was allowed to stick, as he had failed to take the opportunity to express his own thoughts, emotions and points of view.

Recluse, unlike Teflon Man, suffered from an exaggerated reaction to the problems in her relationship with her husband. She was forty-two, a housewife and had two children. She had become accustomed to that role, which for a long time she had disliked – indeed since she had had to give up her job as a secretary on the birth of her first child. She could have reacted at the time, but couldn't manage it, partly in order to fulfil her new status as mother and partly because of her husband's demands. She was almost always incapable of saying no to him. She was a passive-dependant, and she came to consult me in the company of her husband, a salesman of forty-five who regretted that he did not have more time to spend at home with his wife and children. But he also complained of having many worries and that the symptom was complicating both their lives. Recluse was suffering from agoraphobia, so her life was circumscribed by the house and a small garden, and for every trip she had to be accompanied by someone she knew well and could trust. Particularly after the birth of their second child, the symptom gradually took shape, almost as though it were sanctioning her sense of complete impotence and inability to widen the horizons of her life.

The husband, an active-dependant, also underwent a crisis. He had always felt at ease and free to carry out his business, thanks in part to the security he derived from his relationship with his wife. Thus, after the occurrence of this disorder, their relationship as a couple also changed. The anxieties that filled her mind drove her away from intimate and sexual experiences. In spite of the fact that he was attentive, he was clearly tired of the situation that restricted his activities. Recluse sensed this attitude, but could do nothing other than feel guilty and fear that she was losing him. It was necessary to prescribe a pharmacological therapy to bring the symptom under control and give them both greater freedom. But it was also necessary to throw light on the origin of that disorder, which had roots deep in the past and had long been foreshadowed by a form of shyness that she had feared and suppressed.

The examples that we have examined are only three of the possible combinations between psychological and behavioural traits in two partners. As we have seen, the negative effects of bad matches between the four categories concern both partners, to the same extent, although the symptoms are different. This is why it is useful for partners to make an effort to identify which category each of them falls into, and then reflect upon how these interact with each other. Do they produce creativity and togetherness, or misunderstandings and tensions? This could be an opportunity to take an unexpected but salutary look at why certain things happen and are then repeated. It could also be an opportunity to take preventive action against the far from uncommon possibility of shyness in a couple leading to dangerous prostheses and even symptoms.

Aggression

To conclude this chapter on shyness in couples and its effects on relationships, we will examine an element that is far from exceptional in relationships between two people: aggression. If it is a defensive reaction rather than one of attack and expresses itself with more disguised features of submission instead of the more explicit ones of abuse, aggression can represent a means of communication that can belong to the healthy realm of authenticity, but it can also generate various anxieties and even imbalances.

In these latter cases, it expresses a distortion in the love between the partners. In her book *The Bonds of Love*, Jessica Benjamin discusses relationships in which domination plays a major role and there can be no recognition of the other or any rational democracy. Domestic aggression can take many forms. Leaving aside those forms punishable by the criminal code, where the need for domination turns into violence, I would like to examine the more subtle and less conspicuous forms.

First, there are cases in which there is an attempt to keep under control a partner who would otherwise become, it is feared, uncontrollable and threatening. Then there are those in which aggression is suppressed out of fear of revealing too much of oneself and displaying reactions that might be considered reprehensible both in public and in private. The expression of aggression and the inability to moderate one's emotions, feelings and perceptions in a communicative relationship with the other person are typical of those who cannot stand any constructive criticism. Hence they have an often destructive tendency to block off channels of communication and to put up rigid barriers, by abruptly imposing their own point of view. This can occur in many different ways: by demanding the absolute imposition of one's own role; by asserting one's rights as the principal breadwinner in the family; by making a point of who wears the trousers in the house (this could be the woman); and by adopting kinds of behaviour that make it difficult for partners to be close. At first sight, some of these authoritarian attitudes can appear not to belong to aggressive realities, and it is only on closer examination that this becomes clear. This behaviour does not necessarily imply the use of heavy weapons: it is not necessary to raise your fist or shout loudly in order to be aggressive. A cold and detached voice can suffice, as can the neglect of something your partner expects. It can involve the avoidance of sex when you know your partner is aroused.

If you observe this phenomenon in all its forms, there can be no denying that those who express their aggression in certain ways do not display high levels of shyness. Indeed it can be authentic, even healthy, to manifest rising disappointment or anger as it occurs without filtering it out of fear of being sanctioned. However, this can only occur in a fairly narrow area that borders with shyness: somewhere between classically violent aggression and the more subtle disguised form that passes through messages that can even appear plausible at times. For couples, relational problems caused by various manifest or hidden forms of this behaviour are practically the rule. We know that the relationship is really intimate when both partners put all of themselves into it, without fear of being cheated, or worse, being annihilated by the other one and without the desire to cheat or annihilate the other. Such a relationship is one in which there is no desire for domination. This is clearly not an easy type of relationship to achieve in its entirety, given that it involves profound aspects of each partner's psychology. Moreover, the quality of living intimately together is also linked to the degree of stimulation and subduing of positive or negative emotions generated by the relationship.

The more fear invades the field, the more relationships are much more prudently typified by conviviality ('let's stay together because we share interests, friendships and routines') or contractual ties ('let's stay together because we are married or we own a house together'). But fear of what? Of being overpowered, of course, but also of being overpowering; of being destroyed, but also of destroying; therefore fear of aggression, perceived as something so devastating that it cannot be mentioned, except in terms falsified by equivocal language and perhaps through symptoms, as we saw in the case of Failed Athlete, Teflon Man and Recluse. Because of shyness, aggression is taboo in many couples, and goes hand in hand with other taboos possibly relating to sex and intimacy. The taboo is so strong that even just some verbal expression of anger or a temporary loss of control can be perceived as an unbearable threat. The threat is in some general sense meant to be against some profound personal dimensions that trigger fear of losing the object of one's love and the thing on which one feels dependent. For example, of the categories we have examined, the active-dependants and the passive-dependants are the ones who, more than anyone else, are incapable of expressing a healthy aggression. They inhibit and disguise this, just as they disguise their shyness. This is another dimension in which prostheses are the order of the day: often subtle strategies but occasionally a little crude, behind which there is a great deal of hard work, indeed too much hard work, and even anxiety over failure to create the illusion of not appearing shy.

Part Three

Rather than Curing, Caring for Shyness

7   Curing Shyness

Prostheses are either benign or malignant, and the products of a rational adaptation to reality or of harmful amplifications of some profound anxiety. The ones we have examined have displayed the pathologies and near-pathologies of shyness. In itself, the sentiment is in no way an illness. It is a basic part of human psychology and could determine many genuine and authentic expressions, by which it is considered good to tend towards an appearance of invulnerability. Such an attitude could give rise to a virtuous and pleasurable circle on which resoluteness and tolerance (particularly self-tolerance) could be ultimately founded, but unfortunately most individuals do not go down that path. This is why instances where due care is taken of one's shyness are so rare that it becomes inevitable as time passes that symptoms appear requiring treatment.

Today, there is an increasingly pressing need for therapies to deal with shyness, particularly because of the enormous spread of its pathological degenerations. To find our way around the maze of possible cures, it might be useful to take a look at what the market offers shy people. It will be a review that will take us to very different kinds of solutions. Some verge on old wives' tales (and possibly fraud), while others are more reliable. They all give us an idea of the objectives to which the treatment of shyness and its clinical variants aspire. This short review will also show us the situations in which people look for a cure. There are those who want to be treated because they have a real need, but there are also those who want to free themselves of this feeling, solely because they cannot tolerate any weakness in themselves. During this review, I think it is important to bear in mind all the points that have been raised so far. This lodestar will prevent us from becoming overly interested in the treatments for shyness, and will guide us in the final part of the book to another approach to shyness, one that does not want to reject or 'cure' it. For the moment, let's take a look at promises of treatments and cures for shyness.

Sorcerers

At first, it might appear that the sentiment we are concerned with is not the ideal terrain for this particular kind of 'treatment-provider', some of whom ambitiously consider themselves capable of curing it completely. However for one reason or another, many shy people turn to these 'sorcerers' to be cured of their problem or one of its possible manifestations. These people are not just those who suffer from a mild disorder for whom some prosthesis had been working well but is now somewhat less effective. They can include people who are suffering from much more serious forms. They might be oppressed by the need to avoid situations that may also be desirable, they might be crushed by social phobia or they might be terrified of panic attacks with agoraphobia. What they want from their sorcerer is magic and a sudden trick that can free them permanently from that heavy burden. The sorcerer does not shrink from the task and never doubts his ability to respond to demands of this kind. Otherwise, what kind of sorcerer would he be? He generously puts all his art and skill to the job of applying the cure.

Sceptics might turn up their noses at this, but although it is difficult to assess the results, there are some people who claim to have felt better or even to have been cured of their problem through the services of a sorcerer. What is the magic formula by which the burden of shyness can be lifted through such methods? It was explained to me by Disenchanted Dupe who turned to a sorcerer to overcome her social phobia. Following a surprising initial improvement, for which she had paid a considerable fee, she gradually felt all her fears returning. After failure to repeat that good outcome, she decided to turn to a more conventional form of cure. She was a married woman of about forty, her husband was a businessman and she had two teenage children. Having graduated in languages, she worked in the export department of a medium-sized industrial enterprise and lived a somewhat practical life, in which her symptoms stuck out like a sore thumb. She was in no way an incompetent woman.

The idea of consulting a sorcerer was suggested to her by a friend, who fervently believed in such practices and their effectiveness. Disenchanted Dupe explained the strategy used by the man who she hoped would cure her, and as in the best conventional clinic, he examined the causes before planning the therapy. The sorcerer soon identified the origin of her fears, without concerning himself with possible psychological, biological or genetic causes. He told her that it all began when a neighbour put the evil eye on her. That was the cause of all her problems, her fears of other people and her insecurity. The neighbour in question had in fact been around when Disenchanted Dupe's shyness had gradually changed into social phobia. This coincidence gave a veil of credibility to the interpretation. Starting from this 'diagnosis', the sorcerer designed a therapy, while also suggesting a few 'homely' practices for keeping away the negative influences of the tenant on the floor below. The cure turned out to be an amulet, which was specifically prepared for her over a few days, and which, surprise surprise, seemed to work for a time. The woman started to see her friends again, although not in a very relaxed way, but still managing to bear the presence of people she didn't know.

However, the miracle did not last long. It only took the reappearance of her fear in a particular situation to render the amulet useless. Her insecurity proved to be sorcerer-proof. That particular therapeutic practice had used two ingredients that are often the basis of 'magical' practices. The first is to absolve patients of any personal responsibility for their problem and the second is to construct an object that is supposed to act as a kind of crutch: in other words, a prosthesis with magic powers. By attributing responsibility for her symptoms to the neighbour who supposedly influenced her by the evil eye, he removed any direct relationship between Disenchanted Dupe and her difficulties. The causes had been externalized and shifted onto another woman. It only needed some magic practice to keep her at bay, thus freeing the Disenchanted Dupe from the neighbour's negative influence and the anxiety that arose from it. It is well-known that people do not like involving themselves in the resolution of their own irritating problems whose origin is to be found within themselves. It is much better to find a scapegoat and to distance yourself from your shyness and its more negative effects.

This kind of cure also touches on something that shy people instinctively want to do: finding little stratagems and devices for deflecting all negative sensations and avoiding the need to confront a particular aspect of their being. The amulet is nothing more than that. There is nothing magical or miraculous about it: it is simply one more idea in the already varied world of the prosthesis.

Handbooks

Next we leave magic behind us to enter an area with a scientific background, which offers help to sufferers of shyness, although such help is something of a quick-fix. This covers all that technical and popularized literature that aims to provide generally convenient strategies by which the shy reader can understand the cause of the problem and get some good tips on how to solve it. These handbooks are products of the Anglo-Saxon self-help culture, and have been becoming widely used as state contributions to healthcare go down and the costs of health treatment go up, particularly in the United States (in this case we are talking of psychological and psychiatric costs).

So some people have made a virtue of necessity, given that it is not every day that someone gives you useful advice for a small financial outlay. There are many handbooks on shyness, partly because shy people represent a large market, and a great number of them feel the need to overcome their problem. They promise a lot and do give something. They have such titles as 'How To Defeat Shyness', 'How To Find Self-Esteem' or 'How To Get on in the Company of Others'. In general, they don't make excessive claims, given that they are all efforts to summarize various strategies taken from the clinical experience of their authors and made available to their reader-patients. In the majority of cases, therefore, they are worthy undertakings, but they do have one weak point: they recommend artificial behavioural patterns to deal with shyness. These behavioural patterns are similar to the less sophisticated ones that their potential shy readers are already using.

This material is broadly pragmatic. There are at least two variants. The first variant usually leaves a minimal space for individual freedom in finding a way out of shyness. This kind of material is based on thinking that encourages reflection on the concept of self, and the distortions of reality that it has to deal with. Only later do they suggest various levels on which to confront and seek to cure shyness. Handbooks of the second variety are much more prescriptive. Shy people are vehemently exhorted to make up their minds for once and to stop being so chicken-livered. They are subjected to a series of behavioural instructions that completely overwhelm them. For every social situation, there is an appropriate countermove when shyness makes itself felt. They tell you what to say, how to say it and when to say it, as well as giving precious advice for specific situations, such as sex and work. If the reader is astute and follows the lessons conscientiously, then after a certain number of months the battle will be finally won. If unhappily this does not happen, the reason might be that the advice was not so effective after all, but doubts remain that the disciple did not follow the instructions fully to the letter and with the proper commitment.

Handbooks can, as I say, be of some use, if shyness is seen as some kind of weed that has to be pulled up by the roots. This means that it is a diseased part that has to be combated or a weakness with which you unfortunately have to live but which must not be revealed. I am not of the opinion that this is the right approach or winning formula. Indeed, we should consider Freud's view that 'the important thing is not to be cured, but to live'. If you follow the instructions of some handbooks to the letter, it is unlikely that you will be really cured, while it is very probable that you will end up not living as you really could.

Psychiatrists and Psychologists

We have seen that there are types of shyness that can be tolerated after having laboriously constructed some form of prosthesis. However, there are other types that are more evolved or extreme, and they require some adequate form of treatment before the shyness can again be tolerable and compatible with a reasonable quality of personal and relational life. In these cases, attempts to find a cure outside the normal methods are unlikely to succeed. The good advice of handbooks will not be enough, just as an amulet will not cope with social phobia or mitigate the anxiety of someone suffering from evasive behaviour. In these cases, the services of a psychologist and, more especially, a psychiatrist are indispensable in order to cure the ramifications of shyness and the symptoms it generates.

The psychiatrist, in particular, has considerable experience of the clinical situations in which the simple quality of shyness becomes so magnified that it enters a phase in which there are no effective alternatives to control it. Hence the proliferation of psychotropic drugs that can counteract the crippling effects of the more serious pathologies of shyness. In all the variants of social anxiety, this kind of treatment should be prescribed before any psychological treatment, given that the therapeutic effect of the right prescriptions can be rapid and free the sufferer from most of the problem in a relatively short time. Clearly, in such cases it would be somewhat cruel to subject someone solely to psychotherapy with the prospect of positive results over the medium to long term, given that this would leave them prey to their fears for longer than is strictly necessary.

Evidently, those suffering from a 'mild' form of shyness are the least likely to need pharmacological assistance, whereas it is needed by those displaying more serious forms: that includes evaders to some extent, phobics to a greater extent, and those suffering from panic attacks. These people, whose ranks are swelling all the time, are a rich market for the colossal business turnover in psychotropic drugs in general and now the 'new generation' of so-called antidepressants.

However, those who are suitable candidates for these substances should be aware that when a psychotropic drug is used, it is not advisable for the patient to be abandoned to him- or herself. Its use should be accompanied by adequate psychotherapy, so as to strengthen its effects and provide alternative instruments for the patient to use once the pharmacological therapy comes to an end. This caveat is particularly important if you consider that the various 'happy pills' only work on the symptoms and not on the fundamental cause of the pathological process. Indeed, they cannot cure shyness, but tend to alleviate its extreme forms, given that a drug has not been invented that protects you from the fear of others. Bearing this in mind, it should be said that a good number of them have been well-tested, and their biochemical action and effectiveness in alleviating the suffering caused by the most significant symptoms have been proven. They divide into two types: anxiolytics and antidepressants.

Anxiolytics. Anxiety is one of the central features of the various forms of shyness. At first, it might appear logical that anxiolytics, the group of drugs used to control anxiety, are the most suitable for all the manifestations of anxiety that appear in social situations. However, experimental and, above all, clinical experience has shown that, although useful in some cases, they are not the real weapon against these disorders. In fact, the psychological background to all forms of shyness is much closer to the area of mood disorders. As we have seen, the prevailing characteristics concern self-esteem and doubts about one's worth, acceptability and negative dependence in relation to others.

Benzodiazepines, the scientific name for the most widely used anxiolytics, help to reduce some physical manifestations of shyness, such as muscular tension, as well as the subjective feeling of anxiety, but they are not able to help people get over their difficulties in relating to other people. Moreover, they are drugs that, with prolonged use, can lead to dependency. This is so much the case that if their prescription ends, particularly if suddenly, this can cause a 'rebound effect', which means the reappearance of the symptoms for which they were originally prescribed, possibly in a more extreme form.

Antidepressants. You will recall Cloninger's theory concerning the possible nature of our temperament, which was discussed in the first part of the book. As a result of these theoretical considerations, further theories have been developed and research has been carried out leading to the production of a wide range of antidepressants. The temperament types that constitute the biological trademark of shyness, as suggested by the American scientist's theory, depend on the two systems for transmitting impulses to the brain that are called serotonin and norepinephrine. The antidepressants used to treat the more serious symptoms are capable of manipulating these two neurotransmitters. In particular, SSRIs (these act on the serotonin system) and the so-called tricyclicals. This is not the place to discuss the meaning of these two denominations, given that we are much more interested in seeing their effects on some forms of shyness.

All social phobias can benefit from them, as long as the duration of the therapy is sufficiently prolonged (not less than three months) and of an adequate dosage. However, there are some problems. There can be side effects, and there is a risk of the treatment becoming chronic, especially in those cases, which are certainly not uncommon, where termination of the treatment leads to the symptoms returning with their full force. This is why therapies with psychotropic drugs should be reserved exclusively for the most serious cases, while taking the precaution of providing patients with adequate psychotherapeutic help and not leaving them isolated. In all the other cases, they risk becoming nothing more than prostheses whose advantages and disadvantages are now well-known.

Psychotherapy

Although not referring to psychological treatments, Seneca said that a sick person does not need a well-spoken doctor. He was referring to the fact that the most important thing for a doctor is that he knows his trade. In spite of this, it is true that words, the right words that are often a measure of how welcoming a situation is, can be an integral part of curing certain forms of shyness. I don't intend to go into the methods of psychotherapy that are available on the psychic health market. There is a very wide range. Parloff's research in 1979 estimated that there were a 140 types of psychotherapy. Ten years later, further research by Herzing identified 250 types.

Including psychoanalysis, the mother of psychotherapy, every school of thought put forward good strategies for helping patients to free themselves from the problem. If we follow up the reference to Freud, all psychotherapeutic treatments should help patients to develop a good adaptation to their lives, rather than directing them to chase after the hope of freeing themselves of shyness completely. Starting from this assertion, we will look at therapies of the psyche in more detail, taking as an example the so-called short psychotherapies that are very much in vogue. These instruments are characterized by three very clear elements: the limited number of sessions, focused treatment and the limited targets they set. The fact that the number of sessions is fixed right from the beginning prevents the possibility of endless therapies that tend to enter into too many corners of one's existence. In a relatively limited period of time, they aim to assist patients to find a proper basis for regaining health. The treatment is not supposed to have too many observation points, but should be very focused and hopefully agreed between the therapist and the patient. This means the psychotherapy is carried around a pre-established focal point, for instance the relationship with the patient's partner, problems at work, or anxiety in dealing with particular situations. Other elements that might emerge during therapy can then be referred to that focal point.

Moreover, this style of psychotherapy is not used as a kind of archaeology. It is not directed at probing into every conscious and hidden corner of the psyche, every real or imagined event, every memory and every subconscious signal from which to clear material. The objective is restricted to the constructive work, and digging into the distant past is only used for laying useful foundations for the task ahead. The cognitive-behavioural therapies, which follow these guidelines, are generally used for pathologies relating to shyness. They aim to act fairly directly on the patient's thoughts and mental constructs, as well as his or her behaviour. They are based on the premise that the current problems derive from having been unable in the past to learn how to live serenely, and from the mental disorder that this provoked. They therefore attempt to help the patient learn new methods of thought and action. The origin of the patient's difficulties is left to one side, and an attempt is made to identify it and work through it again.

As summarized very well by the French psychiatrists Christophe André and Patrick Légeron in their essay *La peur des autres* ('The Fear of Others'), cognitive-behavioural therapies must help those who suffer from pathological shyness to respond to three problems:

how to stop running away, how to communicate better and how to think in a different way. In other words, the manufacture of prostheses is still required, just as in other therapeutic methods offered by the so-called 'shyness clinics'. The most famous one is in Palo Alto, California. Promotional material for this clinic, whose director is Lynne Henderson and consultant psychologist Philip Zimbardo, outlines the basis on which it operates: 'Shyness and social phobia must not interfere with the achievement of professional and interpersonal goals. The pain of shyness is connected to badly adapted thoughts and beliefs, and new behaviour patterns must be learnt.' The clinic's work follows models aimed at the pursuit of 'mental wellbeing' and 'social adequacy'. It offers a programme that works on five levels: the cognitive (how do I think?), the behavioural (how do I act?), physical control (how do I stay calm?), the emotional (what do I feel?) and the attribution of responsibility (who is guilty?). After six months of treatment, it seems that you can come out transformed into a lion, but there is one nagging doubt: does this mean you'll be king of the forest and free to roam, or will you be caged in another zoo with bars made of different fictions that lead you once again to relinquish a large part of yourself?

Yet they say that the end justifies the means. It is no surprise that attempts to overcome shyness are used to justify a proliferation of ways to disguise it. Leaving aside the criticisms for a moment, these last examples are a little bit more creative. As we have seen, there are more than a few strategies for curing shyness. They are there for those who suffer from it, who feel their throat tighten, who cannot live amongst other people, and who cannot develop plans. They certainly do need help. They need urgent, adequate and hopefully conclusive help. They therefore need to be treated with care and with love. But if they had previously taken care of their shyness, would things have taken a different course? Would they have had to put themselves in someone else's hands in the hope of having chosen the right way to be cured?

8   Remove the Mask!

In the light of what we have seen, the crucial question is not how to confront shyness, but what kind of relationship to have with it. In some cases, there is the wish to eradicate it from one's own psychological territory, and in others, there can be a surprisingly soothing desire to make it one's own, to enter into its full and beneficial possession. To do this, after having taken a long look at prostheses and their significance, and having reviewed all the possible cures for shyness, we need a suitable idea. We need a new idea that finds a way out from the mystification of our psychological reality that is expressed by the use of unconscious stratagems! The new idea also has to avoid turning a pathology into an asset.

Eugene O'Neill provides an interesting metaphor for this perspective in his play *The Great God Brown*, in which he demonstrates the psychological duplicity between the inner monologue and the expression of oneself to others. The characters are provided with masks behind which they hide their faces every time they don't have the courage to express who they are. In particular, a woman called Cybel, who is, as they say, of loose morals, wears the rather common mask of the 'woman-soul', that hides her qualities. These qualities are much more laudable than the ones she actually expresses through her mask. Her true essence can never appear. However, during the play, Cybel has to resort to her mask less and less. What is happening? Simply and extraordinarily, as she gradually allows herself to acknowledge the authenticity of her own instincts (in this case, concerning love), she becomes capable of perceiving and loving what is most beautiful in the man she is getting to know. She is able to appreciate qualities that go beyond possession and the libido, so that no man will ever need to hide behind a mask when in her company. This is a prelude to a new dialectic that does not hide the true essence, the true being of the person involved. Cybel therefore becomes a kind of mirror that gathers a man's desire and returns it to him at the appropriate moment. By relinquishing the need for possession in affairs of the heart, the new-found freedom and the resulting meaningful relationships lead her to project her own personality, her own intimate nature. She can remove her mask and that of the person who comes close to her.

O'Neill is not talking specifically about shyness in the play I have very briefly outlined, but you can interpret an allusion to it in the opening scene and the epilogue. Each mask is distance, obfuscation, and isolation from any authentic links with the world. It encourages those who come into contact with it to provide themselves with a similar instrument and be tempted to negate their own true identity and being. Masks induced by shyness are extraordinary for their capacity to create contrived relationships that border on falseness. They force people to keep their potential qualities hidden, almost as though they didn't exist at all. Someone who lives in a shy manner can therefore never relate to the present. Such people can relate to the past, to nostalgia, to memories, and to the reputation that their existence has gradually produced – a reputation they can never really possess, although, deep down, they always hope they can. They can also relate to the future, to ambitions considered very difficult to achieve, to objectives imposed more by external rules and their own real desires, and possibly to the need to get out of a certain situation to free themselves from feelings of anxiety and fear.

It is as though the present does not exist, as though it does not evolve. It is forgotten and swept away. At the very most, it can be experienced in an artificial manner, as though it were another present and not really part of what is happening. It can be experienced with masks and prostheses, almost as though that precise moment were being experienced by another person and not the real protagonist of that large or small event. So shy people learn to live in another, inappropriate manner, while expending apparent resources that never allow them to relate to themselves. They can never know who they really are, how they could really behave in that present moment, and how in such circumstances their true personality could be accepted and even appreciated.

It is as though they live on the periphery of themselves, without being able to get close to their centre, enter the heart of their own identity, or relate to the secrets that they keep so tenaciously hidden. Yet it is not true that shy people have absolutely no courage. It is not true that they have no resources to display to other people. It is just that they have been trained not to recognize them. This is why it is

ost preferable, to turn to something external in order to
ir shyness. They are so used to hiding behind masks that
tural that they should find other prostheses to cure their
blem. But, as O'Neill has shown, there can come a time when the
mask is no longer necessary and can be thrown aside with a sense of
delight. This is the moment in which the shy person is captured by
the fascination of shyness, and a good relationship is established with
that sentiment made of gentleness and authenticity. This moment
can only be created by the magnificent project of caring for oneself,
for one's own strengths and one's own weaknesses.

9   Caring for Shyness

In order to enter this final and crucial part of our journey through the world of shyness, we first need to put aside our bad habits and fears. Unless it is strictly necessary, we should abandon the temptation to seek out cures for our shyness. Besides, we should ask ourselves realistically whether either magic or science have the instruments to cure it, be they bizarre, empirical, considered or well-tested. The answer could be affirmative if we want to be optimistic, particularly if we give preference to cures with a scientific framework, rather than the more extravagant claims of sorcerers and miracle-makers.

There is indeed a wide variety of remedies. The question then arises of whether science, with its stunning progress, is the right ally in the fight against shyness. So as not to be accused of bias, I will not give a straight no. I will say in all sincerity that scientific discoveries have brought great benefits to humanity, and these have made it possible to cure many illnesses that even recently were incurable. They have allowed extraordinary minds to express their genius, curiosity, determination and love for a particular cause to assist mankind. The truth of this is so clear that only a fool would challenge it.

However, if we apply these basic assumptions to what has been said about shyness, we come up against a weakness in the scientific framework. Scientific research, which is anything but timid, can have little to contribute to this sentiment. It can bring relief to extreme forms of unaccepted shyness, it can cure its transformation into a pathology, and it can treat the forms that have achieved the 'status' of a psychiatric diagnosis, such as the 'personality-evasion disorder', the 'panic-attack disorder with agoraphobia' and 'social phobia'. The feeling of shyness, which is the basis for these pathologies, lost its quality as an integral part of an individual's nature, because it was rejected, mistreated and disguised. It could not bear its lack of recognition and transformed itself into an illness. That feeling of shyness

cannot be cured by science, even in its forms least connected to laboratory science, organic science and psychotherapy. Some schools of
thought can put forward useful instruments and strategies for
producing new ways of masking it, but shyness is still there, hidden
behind the screen and ready to make itself felt when its tenacious
suppression runs into some problem. Then it defies the rules of an
artificial programme.

In the age of cloning and the possibility of reproducing human
beings from a single cell, many psychotherapeutic developments risk
creating doubles, and this brings to mind Dostoyevsky's novel *The
Double*. The Russian writer tells the story of Jakov Petrovic
Golyadkin, a lowly clerk who is 'incapable of being like the others'.
He lives in a state of subjugation to the Tsarist bureaucracy in the
Capital, unable to implement his need to assert and vindicate himself.
Tormented by a sense of moral inferiority and prey to feelings of
persecution, he turns to Doctor Rutenspitz, but is not able to get any
help. In the meantime, he has developed an ambitious project to
marry his boss's daughter, but this desire soon proves quite unattain-
able except in his imagination. Having experienced that it was not
possibly to appear in society without an invitation, this shy and
honest clerk started to do so in the form of his own imaginary double.
This person, who was absolutely identical from a physical point of
view but completely different psychologically, managed by intrigue
and deceit to win the favour of Golyadkin's superiors. He loved and
hated his double at the same time. He was hostile to him and agreed
with him in public. He challenged him to a duel, but felt something
bordering on tenderness towards him. The epilogue finds him, using
a literary device, back in the hands of Doctor Rutenspitz who has him
committed to a home. While the carriage leaves for this destination,
the double waves to him, happily blowing kisses to say goodbye.

As with the shy clerk in Dostoyevsky's story, strategies that
encourage the construction of an imaginary self, a double without a
hint of shyness, can mean losing touch with reality. Of course, this
does not occur in a glaring manner, as with delirium, but with sufficient force to imply an absence of authenticity.

Outside the logic of extreme prostheses and doubles, shyness can
acquire a new form and new significance. It can rediscover its dignity
as a human sentiment and a real part of man's true dimension. This
premise may appear to be something of a paradox, because we are so
used to adopting models that keep shyness at a distance or even ban
it altogether.

In a world governed by image, appearance and illusion, the idea of valuing shyness might even appear inappropriate for these times. I am convinced, however, that in our examination of the various aspects of shyness we have encountered a particular expression of 'serendipity'. We can find this term in the dictionary and its definitions are a good starting-point. My dictionary defines this unusual word, which Horace Walpole coined from the fairy tale 'The Three Princes of Serendip' (an ancient name for Ceylon), as: '1) to find something unexpected and not sought after, while looking for something else; 2) in science, the discovery during empirical observations of data or results that were not predicted by a theory or contradict it, but are of fundamental importance'. The discovery of America is a classic example. While wandering through the pathologies of shyness and the prostheses that it encourages, we might have occasionally thought about the method for removing the causes of those more or less cumbersome effects. Yet, having come this far, while the curative tendency might appear to have the upper hand, something unexpected, important and, to use the dictionary's term, fundamental has appeared before us.

From the somewhat weak mixture of prostheses, pills, handbooks, sorcerers, psychiatrists, psychotherapists and clinics, a different serendipitous theory has been emerging, that is so contrary to received wisdom that it appears to waver between the banal and the blasphemous. It is a simple theory that only requires a change of perspective: a shift of attention away from other people and towards oneself. The theory is this: shyness is not something to be cancelled out, and should not be excluded from the options for character, temperament, and personality. Quite the opposite, shyness is to be praised, not as part of some narcissistic exercise, but as a determined acceptance of one's own reality. If we start to do this, we can finally begin to praise part of ourselves, something that belongs to us and to our authentic dimension.

The psychoanalyst Diego Napolitani, in his preface to Luigi Pagliarani's *Il coraggio di Venere* ('The Courage of Venus'), refers again to that curious word and says

Someone is not 'serendipitous' if they luckily happen upon an event of 'fundamental importance', but only if they have the humility and courage to consider a new and unexpected fact and actively discover the importance, and the extent to which they are willing to abandon the reassuringly narrow path of the theoretical or cultural path along which they are moving when they encounter this new fact.

The book's title suggests a new horizon to someone who is willing to be receptive. The courage of Venus is the courage to relate to one's own beauty. This is not a quality that follows the aesthetic canons, recognized values or demands of a certain circle or society: that is not one's own beauty, it is a required beauty with codified parameters to which you have to conform. It is an ideal of beauty that says, for example, 'thin is beautiful' and helps make it a pathology, as we have seen with anorexia nervosa. You need courage to define yourself in relation to the beauty that is part of you and that you usually ignore out of fear that others will perceive you as something even monstrous, that basic fault that we are accustomed to treating as our unavoidable companion.

This courage is quite simply self-esteem, that love which is respect for oneself, beyond all the contrived practices that we feel are suggested to, imposed upon and required of us. As Pagliarani says, the courage of Venus contrasts with the courage of Mars, just as love contrasts with war, sentiments with aggression, and shyness with all the strategies aimed at concealing and negating it. We can now start to explode the myth that shy people express nothing more than a weak, dangerous and contagious sentiment that has many more vices than virtues.

Making Oneself Presentable

Boris Pasternak has Doctor Zhivago say to Lara: 'Man was born to live, not to prepare himself for life, and life itself, life the phenomenon and the gift of life are a tremendously serious thing! Why replace it with the childish buffoonery of premature innovations?' The question is extremely topical and probably even more pressing today than at the time it was written. The arrival of so much buffoonery, consisting of fickle fashions, ever-changing ideals and the widespread habit of changing beliefs at the drop of a hat, is making the 'business of living' something uncertain in its objectives, its future and its structure. In truth, the mutability of our reference points is generating a sense of life being difficult to live for what it is and how it appears, so that it seems inevitable that we cannot manage to go beyond the interminable preparation to face up to it. For those who are shy this is also true of their own existences, so that they end up living within a cage of hesitations and delays in acting on their real and authentic energies. If there is courage, then it is only the courage of Mars, which is of use in confronting competitive life where there is no place of weakness.

Yet all life is to be experienced, and if you confront it with the right kind of courage, that of Venus, it is a continuous and fascinating voyage of discovery. Of course there are many ways to ruin one's life. There are the more mundane ways: smoking like a chimney, drinking to excess, submitting yourself regularly to every type of stressful event, being too sedentary, chasing after success possibly with little chance of achieving it, always putting your commitments before your pleasures and distractions, taking pills to deal with the effects of stress and other pills to deal with the effects of the first pills, and so the list could go on. Those without imagination can help themselves to as many examples as they want if they read Paul Watzlawick's *The Situation Is Hopeless, but Not Serious (The Pursuit of Unhappiness)*.

There are, however, other strategies for harming oneself and causing visible damage to the quality of one's own existence. Although less striking, they affect the psychological and emotional dimension more than the behavioural one. They manifest themselves as a form of tension and are not always negative. The tension can be positive and perceived as a vital energy that makes us active, productive and enterprising, to use a fashionable term. In these cases, the 'optimal level of anxiety' comes into play, whereby the balance between the performance required and the anxiety provoked is, in a word, optimal. If the level of anxiety is too high, it can generate a state of tension such as to cause paralysis in relation to the required activity, or the sensation of being out of kilter and not having the capacity to deal with the situation. If the tension is too low, demotivation may take over and the lack of incentive to perform the action can make it boring and barely tolerable.

Clearly the optimal level of anxiety is most sought-after in productive systems. It is the level encouraged by motivational courses in companies, which are aimed at optimizing production and creating an emotional energy amongst employees in relation to their work, duties and specific responsibilities. This conforms and indeed pays homage to the current cultural demands. The slogan should be 'Long live tension!' But if you think about it, this device is deceptive: it involves giving up many, too many pleasurable aspects of life to pursue that optimal level. Many things, including your horoscope for the year, have promised that it will bring you lavish prizes, such as fame and fortune. Feelings and emotions manifest themselves differently when shyness is crushed by a number of tensions which individually, if not positive, are at least acceptable, and as we have seen, the effects are not at all similar. They can be over-cautiousness, indecision, withdrawal, remoteness and evasiveness. Such traits are considered contemptible and cannot be displayed in their original form. If they are, you run the risk of being scorned, ridiculed and ostracized in a world that rushes and arrogantly produces. This is the great fear.

If this is the model to which we refer, shyness clearly can only be considered a defect. It is a state to be fought against and eliminated, involving the unpleasant sensation that other people are capable, forceful and successful, while you are inept, incapable and inadequate, just like Charlie Brown, the antihero in Schultz's cartoons. It is as though shy people are short-sighted, long-sighted, astigmatic and hypermetropic, according to whether they are looking at themselves or other people. Thus it is inevitable that they are frightened by a myriad of difficult situations, which they perceive as too taxing for them, their capabilities and their manner of being. Seneca said that it is not that the shy daren't do something because it is too difficult. It only becomes difficult because they cannot dare to do it.

To dare! An unpalatable term, if you follow the logic of shyness that has to be eradicated. You can only dare to do things, if you follow the rules imposed upon you – you can only dare to do things by displaying a double, protecting yourself with some kind of prosthesis, and not showing who you really are. And yet this world that wears a mask appears to be very populous. In his book *Shyness: What It Is, What to Do About It*, Philip Zimbardo states that less than 10 per cent of the population he studied had never experienced social anxiety, tension about being observed, apprehension over putting their own view across and fear of exposing themselves, being criticized and becoming a failure, as if they were constantly having to sit an exam. This means that this research found that nine out of ten people are shy, without taking into account the milder forms of shyness.

However, this does not only apply to our own times. If we look at a few historical figures of undoubted prominence and fame, and not generally associated with shyness, its universality becomes even clearer. Book Seven of *The Odyssey* tells us that even Odysseus hesitated for a moment, suddenly affected by shyness just before being received by Alcinous, the King of the Phaeacians and father of Nausicaa. Erasmus of Rotterdam's *In Praise of Folly* tells us that the leading military and cultural figures who contributed to the greatness of Rome suffered from their doubts. There was a small crowd of them. 'In support of the teacher (Socrates)', he writes, who was facing the death sentence, his follower Plato started to speak. This eminent defender, disturbed by the noise of the crowd, had difficulty in uttering a few mangled sentences. And what of Theophrastus? How could he ever have animated his soldiers in war, when as he rose to speak, he suddenly went silent as though he had seen a wolf? Isocrates, cowardly by nature, daren't open his mouth. Marcus Tullius, the father of Roman eloquence, was often affected by an undignified trembling, and started his speech stuttering like a small boy.

So Napoleon III was in good company, when he hesitated before the Chapel of Tuileries, before entering for Sunday mass and passing through the crowd with everyone looking at him on both sides. This lack of resolution did not go unnoticed. In the times of Greek legend, in the times of ancient Rome and even in the times of the Great Emperor of France, shyness appears to make an exception of very few people. Today, this seems to be even more the case.

But this is not all. It is not just the widespread nature of shyness that makes us wonder why people make such great efforts to hide it and pay such a heavy price. The question has some more personal and private aspects that lead us away from the statistics and put the emphasis back on the individual and his or her self-awareness. It is on this terrain that we come across the serendipity, the wonderful surprise and the coup de théâtre. To help explain myself better, I suggest a geometrical game, whose solution is easily within everyone's grasp, but yet many people cannot manage it. As with shyness, anyone who cannot manage it is in good company and far from alone.

There are nine dots:

The aim is to connect them with four consecutive straight lines, without lifting your pen from the paper. Before reading any further, I suggest that you first try to resolve the problem, given that by discussing its meaning I will reveal how it is done (and in any case the solution appears on the next page). To avoid any confusion, let me say immediately that it does not mean that those who manage to solve the puzzle have necessarily understood everything about life. Maybe they have. But their good performance might only be due to a special knack with geometrical problems, or even prior knowledge of the puzzle that they are not owning up to.

Now let's look at the significance of the problem. Nine dots have to be connected by four straight lines. There is nothing more to it than that. There is therefore a certain margin of freedom. We are not told that the lines have to be drawn within any particular space. Yet it often happens that the space that is considered is strictly limited to the one marked out by the nine dots (and this might have happened to the reader). If you apply this assumption, then you can only keep on trying without ever being able to solve the problem. To succeed, you only need to do something that you are not told you can do but nor are you told you cannot. You just have to realize the possibility of going outside the system, of freeing yourself from the obligation, which does not objectively exist, of being trapped within the pre-established boundaries. In other words, all you need is to allow yourself a little freedom, as follows:

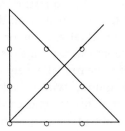

The moral of this puzzle can be guessed at, but it is worth briefly considering it in the context of attentiveness towards oneself, and therefore also one's shyness. This could be instructive. The square marked out by the nine dots metaphorically represents our existential dimension, with its written and unwritten rules – rules that are imposed and others that are incorrectly thought to be rules. In a way, it represents our servility to the norms that are dictated to us, such as the one that says that shyness is contemptible and, less arguably, it needs to be cured when its manifestations become more serious. In this manner there can be no wonderful surprise and no *coup de théâtre*. Everything appears to have been already decided and creativity is suffocated or even reduced to silence.

If we want to adopt a more creative approach to our lives, we need to act very differently. We have to seek out new and imaginative responses to the different situations each of us has to face every day. Rebelling against our shyness is not a creative attitude and only leads to a state of chaos in which the search for pleasure or, more submissively, a little peace, can lead to unhappiness and self-neglect. As in the little puzzle we have just considered, in life we need to go outside the boundaries that appear immutable. You can and it is not prohibited.

This is where we come across the paradox of the metaphor of the game leading to existential questions. Unlike the metaphor, in life and its psychological aspects, you need to go inside the square in order to escape. You need to go towards the centre and not the periphery, towards your inner self, while paying less attention to the world outside. We need to devote attention to ourselves and not to give primary importance to others and their inflexible judgements. In other words, we need a libertarian revolution that prioritizes self-awareness through love for ourselves in contrast to feelings of guilt and fear. All this might appear a theoretical exercise. Yet, if we examine our inner and outer experiences that are contaminated by our shyness, we can assess its practical significance. If we do not respect ourselves, if we assume that we are dominated by the 'basic fault' and if we live in terror of revealing some weakness, doubt or fear, our relationship with the world will inevitably be a distorted one. Moreover, we will not be able to maintain a democratic relationship with ourselves. Hence, our nature, including our true value and qualities, will be so disguised that it will be difficult to decipher or indeed to see at all. In other words, our relationship with reality might not be wholly objective and could be influenced by specific mistaken interpretations.

The Interpretative Errors

Bad habits and practices that perceive the world in an unrealistic manner can become a way of life. Shyness is an inexhaustible reservoir of these interpretative errors. The more you react to them, the more reality is distorted and the greater the errors in interpreting your own role in particular events and in relation to other people. I will list five of them, which I think you should go over while keeping to the forefront of your mind the central theory that by nurturing your shyness many of these mistakes can be avoided.

1. 'All or nothing' thoughts. These reflect the tendency to consider events to be either absolutely positive or absolutely negative. There are no intermediary gradations, so that fear of failure leads to trying too hard and trying to prove absolute ability to do what appears to be needed. Such thoughts accompany the lives of those who perceive their shyness as the expression of their negative side, something so ugly that it has to be suppressed by any means, as long as such means are admired by others and conform to their values.

2. Selective interpretations. These cause an inability to take any risks. When faced with some event, project or innovation, those who fear failure become faint-hearted, as only the possible negative effects come to mind. Hence they cannot make a positive choice and do not consider the possibly positive outcomes. Because of their fear of failure, shy people risk being tied down and force themselves to keep their needs and desires in limbo with no hope of being gratified. They do not give themselves any choice, except on those rare occasions when there is the certainty of no risk of incurring disapproval.

3. The tendency to 'self-deprecation'. This is an exquisitely psychological question. It is the tendency of those who cannot manage to have a reasonable relationship with their own qualities and anything they create. Their shyness often leads them to undervalue something worthwhile that they have produced. This is the clearest manifestation of aesthetic anxiety. When we are praised or valued, we are more exposed to others and visible to their scrutiny. This theoretically pleasurable and gratifying circumstance, in which you reap the rewards of your commitment and hard work, can become unbearable for shy people. Their lack of self-esteem can make them fear that, in such an exposed position, they could find themselves in a situation where others could perceive their secret or defect that must never be revealed. The wonderful opportunity is transformed into a disaster. This is why they tend to minimize their achievements, to hide their involvement in their creations, and to detract from their value.

4. Perfectionism. Shy people are masters of this field. As they are never free to live at a pace that suits them, they amplify the demands they feel are made upon them, and feel that they have to fulfil them to the full. This is the dimension of shyness that leads those who experience but cannot tolerate it to seek absolute targets – something that comes close to perfection. Perfectionism can become a prison sentence. By following the instructions of the ideal Ego, of that projection of oneself inexorably driven to ever bolder enterprises in the hope of finding some suitable recognition, they consume their energies and resources without ever feeling satisfied. Their shyness, which they refuse to accept, becomes caught up with a fragile self-esteem that prevents them from feeling any form of real pleasure.

5. The mistaken attribution of cause and effect. The repression of shyness can lead to a wide variety of elaborate tricks to avoid being exposed. There are even some shy people who reach the point of denying the patently obvious. There has been a success. Well, why not accept your credit for it? The causation would appear appropriate, obvious and obligatory. But no, this cannot be allowed to happen. There are those who react with so much shyness that they attribute the good result to luck, a series of favourable circumstances or the benevolence of their God. Of course, one might say this is just a modest and slightly reserved person. After all modesty and discretion should not be criticized. This is true, even though our hypothetical shy person is paying slightly too high a price for them, but if we follow him or her into other difficult situations, the results can be more disturbing. On another occasion, the same individual finds that everything goes wrong. Bad luck? Unfavourable circumstances? No, nothing like that. The failure is entirely his fault, and he takes complete responsibility for it. He attributes it to his own ineptitude, and feels a complete loser. When does such a person have a chance to enjoy fully his own existence?

Shyness has left its mark on all five errors. It is concealed, suppressed and masked, and yet it is still able to jump back out again. They may not be particular symptoms or pathologies, but they are a series of major annoyances and create a lifestyle structured in such a manner that there is no room for pleasure, serenity or peace. These interpretative errors have shown us once again where the lack of courage to express who we are can lead us. If we allow them to take over our lives, we will ban shyness and fail to nurture it. Because they are as widespread as shyness itself, and because they are accompanied by prostheses of varying degrees of effectiveness, a great mass of men and women must have excluded the courage of Venus from their psychological patterns and therefore from their lives. Hence work upon the interpretative errors is one of the specific direct or indirect tasks of all psychotherapies, but it might be asked whether it is absolutely necessary to deal with them in order to nurture one's shyness.

We have seen that it is occasionally useful and even necessary, but it can be avoided by those who want to approach a different method with conviction. Let me stress again that nurturing your shyness is above all a question of taking care of yourself, but it is also something more. It is an excellent preventive measure against its pathological forms.

10   Playing with Shyness

If you are careful to avoid the traps just referred to and whose form and content we have examined, it will certainly be less difficult to structure a more gentle relationship with your own shyness. If you lay down the arms you use to fight it, there may come a time when you are reasonably at peace with and tolerant of yourself. But this is not all. People who have lived under the obligation to live up to a lifestyle with a constantly competitive flavour, will be able to start to relax. They no longer have to struggle under the terrible weight of imagined rules that incessantly demand success. So much less hard work!

You can then go down a different road that is encouraged and mapped out by the pleasant attentiveness you show to your shyness. It can have the agreeable feel of a game. In order to explain myself, I have to return to the chapters on prostheses. It is not possible to play with the ones that have toxic ingredients, such as aggression, drugs, pathologies or withdrawal. They all script an unsuccessful attempt to ostracize shyness. However, many other prostheses can be transformed into instruments for which playfulness is attainable for everyone.

Pain-in-the-Neck was an example of this. People feared his explosive capacity for turning an everyday conversation between friends into a vicious argument. A mild, well-mannered and generous man, his problem when we met was that he suffered from premature ejaculation. When he was thirty-six, the symptom started to get worse and, as his marriage got into difficulties, he decided to do something about it. It was not only sex that was not going as he would have wanted; he also had problems in his relationships with other people. He could never relate to them in a serene manner, and was always in a state of anxiety. The result was that he turned even the most commonplace discussion into fierce debate. His verbal outbursts were a public transformation of the disorder he suffered deep inside:

his inability to create an agreeable distance between himself and others, and an appropriate pace for his relationships. He feared other people and got in first before he felt exposed. In spite of everything, his generosity and availability had stopped him from being completely cut out of his group of friends. Nevertheless his presence did create a certain unease. Having alleviated his difficulties with his wife and resolved his sexual problem through a period of therapy as a couple, we then turned our attention to his way of keeping people at a distance. Pain-in-the-Neck became a former pain in the neck in every sense of the term. In truth, his shyness was not in the least modified, but he learnt to play with his prosthesis, once he had acknowledged it and identified its function.

Instead of seeking argument at all costs, he became the 'critical mind' of his group of friends, with a new style that finally did justice to his true character. His argumentativeness became a game by which he still controlled the others a bit, but without the fear and negative tension that made him express himself aggressively. In this new way of expressing his own prosthesis, he could appear friendly and charming to his companions. He was simply more relaxed and relating to his shyness in a different and more benign manner. The case of the former Pain-in-the-Neck shows that it is not always necessary to dispose of one's prosthesis in order to nurture one's shyness.

Advertising recommends the use of prostheses. One advertising slogan claims 'People say that chewing-gum increases self-confidence.' By this it means that if you are shy and insecure, you are obliged to do something to increase your forcefulness so that you can face the world. However, we have to ask ourselves whether prostheses really should be considered means to attain success at all costs, to assert oneself in some way and to equip oneself adequately to respond to other people's demands, or whether they could be used with a certain degree of irony. In other words, we can use status symbols, we can go over the top with our jokes in order to gain a prominence that otherwise would not be conceded, or we could undergo the plastic surgeon's knife, as long as these types of decision come within our area of self-awareness. This means awareness that the earnest, heavy and emotionally tiresome tone used for masking shyness can be transformed into a pleasant game. Prostheses can then become agreeable, even amusing instruments, as long as they are not used for subjugating loneliness, fear or other people.

The need to succeed makes life difficult for shy people. The continuous competition imposes a level of stress and hard work that can never produce anything worthwhile. In the climate created by such a perspective, there is no room for play, and the obligation is also to take yourself seriously. You can never allow the introduction of this disturbing but also fascinating sense of shyness into your fun. By defending your shyness (rather than defending yourself from it), you are simply creating greater freedom in your relationship with others, without preconceived ideas or the rejection of the pleasure in an innocent prosthesis.

Indeed there is nothing wrong in wearing a mask, as long as it is done in a carnival atmosphere and with the freedom to remove it. Just as with the playfulness of carnival day, revealing one's face is part of the fun in the company of others. Too often shyness deprives us of our sense of humour, making us easily offended to the point of making ourselves disagreeable. Playing with shyness can make us more thoughtful and less anxious. It can give us the time before responding to decide what is best and to deal with a compliment that otherwise would have embarrassed. Prostheses without playfulness are directly opposed to the purpose for which they were originally intended. They create distance and even disapproval: the very reactions that the shy person wishes to avoid. In order to nurture your shyness, you need to break out of the malevolent logic of its concealment and enter the benevolent one of its creative manipulation, as though it were clay in a sculptor's hands. To use shyness properly, to return it to its role as an integral part of yourself and your nobility, you have to allow some of its properties, which retain something of childhood, to enter the scene, without fear of appearing childlike and therefore being disapproved of.

You need to go back and exploit the origins of your shyness and to the time it came to maturity, in order to give it the dignity it deserves. It is no longer a fault, but an aspect of your own development. Playing with shyness or, if you like, in spite of your shyness, also means no longer being frightened of becoming slightly childlike. The use of prostheses, whether good or bad, to fight, hide or destroy shyness is the use of heavy and inappropriate weapons against your own past, against your own development and against the formation of your own personality. Those very events have made you unique and unrepeatable, and precisely for this reason, we all have something exceptional and valuable about us, as long as we allow ourselves to see it.

11 Conclusion

I cannot be certain whether, having come this far, you are really convinced that shyness has its fascination or whether you continue to fear it and to feel it pressing down on you. Perhaps you have at least started upon the rewarding journey. It is not easy to change our personal rules and the parameters of self-evaluation. It is difficult to sweep away the waste material and deposits of bad old habits. Many people might still be tempted to interpret the reality that surrounds them in an incorrect manner. They may still fall into the trap of attaching too much importance to a particular event, while undervaluing another. They may be hard on themselves or see things in black and white terms. They may suffer the allure of perfection or have difficulties in being in the company of others.

If we observe this great multitude of people and their tendency to engage in these confusions, we may wonder whether these attitudes are nothing more than normal human reactions and behaviour. As such, there should be no need to define them as abnormal, reprehensible or indicative of excessive weakness. Indulgence and understanding can then prevail. Thus shyness in others can cease to appear a source of particular fears or something particularly charming. It is widespread in its concealed form and widespread in its extremely explicit form. The same indulgence we adopt towards others should also be adopted towards ourselves. But it is anything but typical for us to do this. When we need to think about our own identity, not necessarily in relation to the supposedly successful but simply to those who are different from us, then there is a serious risk of wanting to hide ourselves. Yet diversity means nothing more than managing your own life in your own particular way in relation to your own qualities and defects, strengths and weaknesses, and areas of security and insecurity.

As Paolo Flores d'Arcais has written in the Dictionary of Philosophy produced by the Italian current affairs magazine *MicroMega*:

> The individual is *unrepeatable*. A world populated by individuals is therefore a *plural* world made up of unrepeatable pluralities. To support individualism is to champion the right of anyone to be an I, to say I and to be the protagonist of a life that is irremediably and unalienably his or her own. 'Individual' does not mean One, but *each of us*. It implies a perspective that stubbornly upholds an *obsessive* equality of dignity and worth.

This fundamental concept should make us reflect on how devastating it is to withdraw from the core of our own being in order to relate to others in a manner that we think they expect, using prostheses also aimed at the supposed gratification of their expectations. In this way, we create many problems. It affects the way we treat our shyness, causes us to neglect it, and can make us live not as we would like or as we could, but as we think others expect us to.

It is true that occasionally by some strange and subtle magic the fear of censure and disapproval can induce us to act in a manner that is valued. But in this case, can we really have self-esteem and self-respect when we have to acknowledge that it wasn't our true nature that people liked but a prosthesis? We run the same risk as Gaines, the protagonist of a story by Charles Bukowski, who while looking at his reflection in the mirror, says: 'I *seemed* to be someone who knew something. What tripe, I was a fraud, and there's nothing worse in this world that a man who suddenly discovers that he's a jerk, having spent his life trying to convince himself that he is not.'

Finally, when are we going to have this meeting with ourselves and a true relationship with our own identity? When are we going to reclaim our own uniqueness in this world of mass culture that demands stratagems and masks that make everyone the same, everyone without doubts, fears or shyness? I am convinced that nurturing your shyness in today's world is a truly innovative and anti-conformist perspective that denies the conventional wisdom that leaves no room for inner strength, but only aggression, ambition and well-developed muscles. It alone can bring back a reasonable level of spontaneity, and put human relations back on the road that not only tolerates differences, but values them. A world in which everyone could, without fear, nurture their own shyness, without the need to mask it, would not only be a better world, but could create a great psychological and cultural revolution which would take us away from mythologies and mass utopias, and return us to the ideology of the individual as the precious centre of the world, with all his or her own qualities and defects.

This is the only route to the final realization of the need to do away with masks, prostheses and the exorcism of shyness. This aim is both ambitious and easy to achieve, as long as you put the most emphasis on valuing yourself and accepting every part of yourself, be it strong or weak, beautiful or ugly. Only by starting to first tolerate and then nurture aspects of ourselves that we feel to be irretrievably defective, can we discover the qualities, richness and beauty that belong to us. If we want to negate what appear to be reprehensible and vile emotions, if we want to reject our shyness, we will inevitably end up denying our own existence and dignity. If we were to leave aside the stereotypes that produce prostheses, we could probably enter into a new type of dialogue.

This is what happened in the case of two shy and tolerant revolutionaries. Very probably there were more than two: maybe ten, but some say there were a hundred. They happened to read in a newspaper advert Marshall McLuhan's assertion that 'Advertising is the greatest art form of the twentieth century.' Without warning, they signalled their complicity and, almost in unison, they felt an expression of doubt escaping from their mouths: 'Do you really think so?' And they laughed, each blushing slightly at that sacrilegious doubt. But naturally they didn't care, now they realized that there were so many people like them. The well-informed tell me that there were many thousands.

Bibliography and Further Reading

American Psychiatric Association, *Diagnostic and Statistical Manual of Mental Disorders*, Fourth edition (Washington DC: A.P.A., 1995).

ANDRÉ, C., LÉGERON, P., *La peur des autres* (Paris: Odile Jacob, 1995).

ANDREOLI, V., *Giovani* (Milan: Rizzoli, 1995).

BALINT, E., BALINT, M., *The Basic Fault: Therapeutic Aspects of Regression* (London: Tavistock Publications, 1983).

BAUDRILLARD, J., 'Du bon usage de la séduction', *Quaderni di Sessuologia Clinica*, III, 2/3, 3–8, 1984.

BENJAMIN, J., *The Bonds of Love* (London: Little, Brown, 1990).

BIANCHI, M.B., *Andy Warhol. Aforismi mai scritti* (Viterbo: Millelire Stampa Alternativa, 1994).

BRUCH, H., *Conversations with Anorexics* (Jason Aronson, 1988).

CROOK, M., *The Body Image Trap: Understanding and Rejecting Body Image Myths* (Bellingham: Self-Counsel Press, 1992).

FREUD, S., *Sigmund Freud, Vol. 7 – On Sexuality*, ed. by A. Richards (London: Penguin Books, 1991).

GINDIN, R.L., 'The Penis Dreamed by Patients, Physicians and Sexologists – Looking Beyond the Perfect Penis', XII World Congress of Sexology, Valencia, 25–29/6/1997.

KOHUT, H., *Analysis of the Self: A Systematic Approach to the Psychoanalytical Treatment of Narcissistic Personality Disorders* (London: Hogarth Press for the Institute of Psycho-Analysis, 1971).

LOWEN, A., *Joy: The Surrender to the Body and to Life* (London: Arkania, 1995).

MANARA, F., *In coppia per amarsi* (Milan: Sperling & Kupfer, 1996).

MARSHALL, J.R., *Social Phobia: From Shyness to Stage Fright* (New York: Basic Books, 1995).

NOVELLI, M.E., *Psicologia della vergogna* (Rome: Edizioni Universitarie Romane, 1986).

PAGLIARANI, L., *Il coraggio di Venere* (Milan: Raffaello Cortina, 1985).

PANCHERI, P., *Lo stress in psichiatria e in psicosomatica* (Rome: Il Pensiero Scientifico, 1982).

PASINI, W., *La qualità dei sentimenti* (Milan: Mondadori, 1991).

PASINI, W., *I tempi del cuore* (Milan: Mondadori, 1996).

SAGAN, E., quoted in MCKAY, M., FANNINO, P., *Self esteem* (Oakland: New Harbinger Publisher, 1992).

SELYE, H., 'The Evolution of the Stress Concept', *American Scientist*, 61, 692–6, 1973.

VOLTERRA, V., 'Gli interventi psicoterapeutici nel trattamento del disturbo di panico', in the conference acts of *Congresso dal temperamento alla malattia*, held in Pisa on 21/2/1997.

WASSMER, A., *Making Contact* (Magnum Books, 1995).

WATZLAWICK, P., *The Situation Is Hopeless, but Not Serious (The Pursuit of Unhappiness)* (New York: W.W. Norton, 1993).

ZIMBARDO, P.G., *Shyness: What It Is, What to Do About It* (Reading Mass.: Addison-Wesley, 1990).

Index

Compiled by Sue Carlton